Loss, Life, Love
By Nalanie Harilela Chellaram

Edited by Les Anand Roberts

Note to Readers: This book is intended solely as a practical guide to help people go through the trauma of bereavement. As such it is not to be considered as a substitute for formal and professional counselling either in respect of bereavement or any other emotional issue, or any form of mental health treatment or therapy, as provided by suitably qualified professionals. The case studies referred to herein are factual, and the advice given to patients (referred to as 'clients') during consultations was tailored to suit the individual and unique circumstances of each case. Readers are therefore advised to seek proper professional help where appropriate and necessary, and where such professional help is warranted but not sought then neither the publisher, the printer nor the author can accept any responsibility or liability for any claims or damages whatsoever and wheresoever arising.

In addition, this book is based upon and relates various Yogic practices and tenets belonging to the Hindu tradition as taught by Sri Swami Satchidananda and other Great Sages, and various quotations herein are primarily drawn from Hindu texts. However, in keeping with the ethos and motto of the Integral Yoga Organization that 'truth is one, paths are many', the author, the printer and publisher fully respect all faiths, beliefs and religions.

Printed in the United Kingdom

First Edition

ISBN 978-1-80049-081-9

Printed by Acorn Press, Westmead Industrial Estate, Westmead Drive, Westlea, Swindon, SN5 7UU, United Kingdom
www.acornpress.co.uk

Cover design by Natasha Bacarese-Hamilton

Dedicated

To Shanky
For teaching me about life and death

To Shani & Andrew, Shaman & Hersha
For always being there for me

To my grandchildren Tara, Natasha, Talia
Indira & Shahan
For being the lights in my life

To my parents George & Chandra Harilela

To my siblings
Mira, David, Maj, Kumar, Kantu & Lavi

And to my darling Les
For bringing me from sorrow back to joy

Acknowledgements

I am deeply indebted to my partner, Les Roberts, for his support and encouragement, and for overseeing the editing of this book, and most of all for his love. Following the passing of my husband of 34 years, Shanky, in 2008 I entered a dark period of mourning through which I was sustained by my faith in God and by my spiritual practices. And then Les came into my life and I realised it was possible to love him and still hold that special place in my heart for my late husband. Now Les and I work together, laugh together and share common goals, to serve, love, give, meditate, purify and realise!

My sincere gratitude also goes to Julio Alcantara, my spiritual brother, for writing the foreword and for sharing his experiences following the loss of his beautiful wife and soul-mate, Paddy San; to Turttu Balson, Georgia Bizzell and Yolanda 'Chitra' Alvarez who kindly agreed to contribute their personal stories; to my good friends Avisha, Kim and Ole, Luckshmi Marina, Sylta and Ulla, and to Paddy and Jennie Crouch for proofreading and for printing this and other books for me; to my PA Susanna 'Shanti' Alman for all her assistance; to all the members of both the Gibraltar and Spanish Sanghas for their love, support and dedication; to the members of the Gibraltar committee, past and present, who have supported the Yoga Centre and made it function so well, in particular Lilian Shaw, Namrata Tulsidas Gulraj, Michele Dumoulin, Anju Budhrani, Rosanne Torillo, Cynthia Walker, Gigi Britto, Daya Dewfall and Tony Sacramento, and to Anna Triay; to Swami Karunananda, Swami Gurucharadananda (Mataji) and Prem Anjali from Yogaville; and to all my 'patients' who taught me so much! Thank you everyone, I am so blessed to have you all in my life!

And finally, I am unbelievably indebted to my beautiful Spiritual Master, Sri Swami Satchidananda, for all the teachings He patiently and lovingly passed on to me, opening my eyes to God, to the Divine Consciousness within me and within everyone and everything. This book is both a tribute and a testimony to His words of wisdom, His philosophy and the spirit of oneness encapsulated in the motto of the Integral Yoga Organisation He founded, that *truth is one, paths are many.*

And thank you my beautiful granddaughter, Natasha, for the cover design.

Contents

It is very difficult to define my relationship to this beautiful soul, Nalanie. I have known her for well over thirty years throughout which she has been my dearest friend, my mother, my sister, my guide. Life has brought us together so that I might share in the joys, the sorrows, and the pain of our time on this earth through the teachings of our beloved Gurudev, her family friend and spiritual Master, Swami Satchidananda. Twice at critical and deeply painful times in my life, Nalanie was the Light that took me out of the deep dark cavern of hopelessness and grief. In the first, she gave me back my beautiful, vibrant Paddy, lost in the thick fog of depression, that curse of modern life. More recently, sinking with the heavy, painful burden of loss, she extended her hand, her love, and her guidance, to lift me out of my own murky sea of bereavement and depression.

Thanks to her, my dearest Paddy and I were able to embark on a life's journey of great adventure and beauty, giving us direction and a new vision, through the science of Yoga.

But, good teaching is not what you say, but what you do and how you do it. I can vouch for the truth of what she writes; for the truth of how she lives her life. Myself a teacher, I have never seen a spiritual teacher so painfully tested in what she affirms, in what she believes. I watched closely the unfolding, relentless drama of my dear friend Shanky's passing away. I have seen and felt her pain and shared in her sadness. Yet, through her, I have also seen the power of a deep, unshakeable, faith; faith in the fundamental goodness of the Cosmic Consciousness – God's Plan is Perfect! It is this protective shield of Light and Love that she wants to share with us through this book, reliving her life, and told openly with quiet gentleness. We manifest our love of God when we share it with those seeking to grow in the love and compassion of the Oneness of Creation. "Loss, Life, Love" is but one sharing.

"When you see the stainless unity of God everywhere, you become established in Brahman and rise above the constant changes of this world."

(The Holy Bhagavad Gita: Chapter 5 - Sloka 19)

Loss, Life, Love
Preface

I had read many books about death and dying. I had contemplated the subject often. I truly understood that we all die. I myself had been on my deathbed four times. I had lost my beloved Dad and my great Guru, Swami Satchidananda, the two people I admired most in my life. Yes, I was truly saddened and missed them but I was totally prepared with all the knowledge I had. I realised they were of a ripe age and life took them at the perfect time. Since then two of my siblings have also departed. Mira aged 69, who was really like a Mom to me, and my brother Kumar aged 67, a kind, gentle soul to all. Many friends have left this earth since. One in particular, our dear Paddy 'San' Alcantara who served tirelessly at the Gibraltar Yoga Centre and was my personal assistant, struck the heartstrings of my soul deeply. Strong connections. All too young. All deaths from cancer.

When it came to the death of my beloved husband Shanky, I was shell shocked by the tremendous pain. I felt that someone had torn my soul apart and that part of me was just dead, just gone. The horrendous pain literally gnawed at my heart constantly without abate especially for the first six weeks after he passed. After that I had periods of peace. These short bursts of pain release came only when I was not absorbed in my own sorrow. They came when I forgot myself and just dived into my work. My children and grandchildren were the lights in the darkness for me; their innocent charm lifted me from my deep sorrow.

When the ache started to lift after the first six weeks I felt that I was going through some kind of metamorphosis. I had no idea what was happening. I just knew that something in my psyche was shifting. Good or bad, I was not sure. I was just aware of a letting go. Life seemed so surreal and nothing appeared so important anymore.

There was a softness that emerged from that pain; a compassion so profound for anyone who had suffered a loss. A desire to serve them and help them in any way I could. A feeling that suffering was my teacher and not a punishment. I had to help others free themselves from this cage of darkness.

There was an inner voice compelling me to write this book. To serve those who had lost such loved ones. To give them signposts to relieve the pain and to understand the healing that has to take place in order to make sense of life. To give hope to those who feel lost and laughter to those who shed all those millions of tears.

My husband and I had been married for 34 years. I always said the best years were after the 25th. That's the truth. That is the absolute truth. It became even better because I had learned the science of Yoga, the science of learning about oneself, the science of looking within, of finding divinity within. I think that science gave me the opportunity to love my husband as I could and should have loved him. It all helped me to be more selfless. Prior to this science I was extremely selfish and I never knew it. I never saw it. I only began to realise it when I started to meditate and watch myself, because you do start to observe yourself when you get in touch with your spirit. When you go deep within, you start to experience that you are spirit, and when you start to experience that you are spirit there is a gift that comes to you, to all of us, nobody is exempt. And that gift is the ability to watch the way you think.

Once you know how you think then it is your choice whether you have the courage to change it, to be brave enough to change it. It is the ego that stops you. It is pride that loves to place blame on someone else. You consider yourself holy just because you are the one practising meditation and doing yoga. A tragic mistake! We are *all* holy. We just forgot to be 'whole'. To be whole is to merge with all Consciousness in everyone and everything.

In writing this book I want to relay my own personal experience with death and how I dealt with bereavement, and ultimately came through it. I hope it will help those who have lost someone, or who are experiencing the terminal illness of someone close. You can never explain it to anybody else until you go through it. People will tell you that they know how you feel, but very often you know that they don't know. And it doesn't really matter. It's not really important. What is important is how you live and deal with these circumstances. Understand that those suffering from a terminal disease may be very bad tempered. It's normal and we must have so much compassion for them. Give to them all the love you can and every time they scream or shout at you know it is because they're unwell and fearful. Think 'God is teaching me compassion. The Lord of love is teaching me patience and empathy'.

Someone called me a few weeks after my husband had left on his onward journey and said, "Nalanie, I was thinking that you must be filled with regret for all the things you never said to your husband or did with him". I thought it rather presumptuous and lacking in awareness. However, I answered, "There was never any guilt or regret. We spoke a lot and we had total closure".

The thought running in my mind was 'Dear God, I am so grateful that you gave me the strength to give my husband a beautiful passing. Of course I miss his strong presence and I am in great pain but you Lord gave me the strength when I needed it most, and which enabled him to leave his body peacefully and with incredible dignity'.

Shanky passed in December 2008 after a mercifully brief battle with cancer. My spiritual journey began in 1987 when I was 33 years old and continues to this day – and will continue until I, like Shanky, shall move on to 'the other side'.

Nalanie Harilela Chellaram
Andalucia Spain
September 2020

Loss, Life, Love

Book One

Loss

The phone rings.

"Cough, cough, cough, cough."

"Darling. What's wrong? Why are you still coughing?"

"It's nothing, Honey. It's the same cold I had when you left. Just taking a little longer to get better. I went to the doctor yesterday and he gave me something stronger."

"But it's been too long and you're really hacking. I'm worried."

"Nothing to worry about. I also went to see Peter Borge and he has given me some steroids so I should be fine in a day or two."

"Oh great. That always does it for me when I have a bad cough. I know Peter will look after you."

"Okay, I've got to go. Shani is here and I've got to make dinner. Okay, darling, bye-bye."

I'm very uncomfortable. I don't know why. There's a pain in my gut. I almost want to throw up. But I can't and I don't have time for myself now. I've come to the States because Kantu's husband has been diagnosed with stage three pancreatic cancer. Kantu is my sister and I love her dearly so I've come to New Jersey to help her. I have only come for twelve days. I tell myself, Nalanie, stop over-thinking and focus on Kantu. My husband, Shanky, is in good hands. Dr Peter Borge has been more than a family doctor. He's been a close friend for years and has been my saviour in the past whenever I have had an asthmatic attack. Besides, our daughter, Shani, is with Shanky and she's strong and smart, and can take care of her Dad while I'm away.

Kantu and I had plans for that day to drive to the hospital, as her husband, Vijay, was due for his chemotherapy treatment. We walk into the hospital and into the room where he is to be given his chemo intravenously. There is a gloomy and dark feeling all around. About six people are scattered around the room. The nurse is trying to cheer them up and I can see a feeling of dread on all of their pale, grey faces. The smell of death hits me. The smell of sickness and that same nauseous feeling overcomes me.

I turn around and smile at Vijay and Kantu. I am here to lift their spirits, not to focus on the darkness. So we sit Vijay down for his treatment. Over the next few hours, we pass the time joking with him, and laughing. When the session is over, we go for lunch, but he looks drawn and grey and has lost all interest in eating. I see that my sister and he are avoiding any conversation that has any depth, any depth at all, about mortality, life and disease. There is not even talk about hope. It is like everyone is pretending that nothing is happening, and yet everything is happening.

The following few days with my sister, I watch how she tries to cope. She's developed a bit of OCD, trying to clean all the time. I catch her at midnight scrubbing the toaster and mopping a very clean floor. I stop her.

"What on earth are you doing?"

She bursts out crying.

"Sis, we need to talk. We need to talk about your husband's illness and how you are feeling. Are you scared?" I ask her.

It is clear she is petrified, but doesn't know who to tell and what to say. Suddenly with anger, she shouts, "He's not going to die, he is going to live."

"It's great that you have hope. I'm so happy you have hope, but at the same time you need to deal with what is going on."

We chat until the early hours of the morning and I try to explain to her that during these times, these moments with her husband, she needs to be more aware of their existence together and what he really needs.

She goes to bed. I think she feels truth in my words, but she is afraid to really hear them.

The next day, Vijay looks exhausted. He is sitting on his favourite armchair. He tells me that his legs are hurting so I ask him would he mind if I massaged them.

He smiles and says, "I would love it."

I massage his legs, laugh with him and ask, "Vijay, is there anything you would like to talk about?"

"Yes, my wife," he replies. "Oh, Nalanie, she is really my angel. She's been with me from the beginning. She's helped me bathe when I couldn't do it after chemo. When I've fainted, she's picked me up. She takes me to the doctor; she's by my side. But, at the same time, whenever she can, she avoids me. She starts cleaning. And I'm a bit confused by all of this. Please, can you speak with her and tell her not to clean so much? I'd like her to talk to me."

I bring my sister into the room so I can speak to both of them. I tell Kantu what Vijay had shared with me. They hold hands. I teach her how to massage his legs. I love the feeling of peace that comes over his face, a gentleness, and a look of release on my sister's face. They were communicating. There was something deeper now.

The following day my husband calls again and I hear the same hacking cough.

"You're not better darling. Maybe we need to see another doctor."

"No, no it's only been a day or two, Nalanie. It will be fine. I have to go now because I need to pick up our granddaughter from school. I love you very much."

"Should I come home, darling?"

"Don't be silly, you will be home in a few days. You went to help your sister and that is what you are there for. Your brother-in-law has cancer. I'm fine, I just have a cough."

The next few days with my sister and brother-in-law are very intense as I bring up the subject of death, which is really hard to do, because I know they are averse to even thinking of it. At first they resist the conversation.

Vijay says firmly, "I'm not going to die."

I smile and reply, "What are you talking about? We are all going to die one day, all of us! None of us are spared. We are born alone and we die alone. All I am suggesting is that you prepare. My philosophy is 'prepare for the worst, but know the best could happen'. In fact, just before I came to you, Shanky and I were discussing how we wanted to word our will, and we plan to organize it once I get home."

I sense anger projected at me. Reality and truth sometimes are so hard to accept. I understand that the anger is coming from fear. They are my family and I love them. Fortunately, the next day I am due to go to the Satchidananda Ashram in Virginia, and I can leave them alone to work things out in their own minds; to understand the real nature of the disease and how they could help themselves get through this without burying the truth.

I arrive at the Ashram and Prem Anjali, the former secretary of my guru Sri Swami Satchidananda (who left the body in 2002), greets me. She has arranged accommodations for me that are private, quiet and away from the main hub of the Ashram. How does she know? How does she know that I would greatly benefit from this quiet time with my spirit before going home to my husband?

The next three days at the Ashram are magical and very hard for me to explain in words. I feel the power and the energy of the vibrations of my beloved spiritual Master. It feels like pins and needles are being pushed into my body all of the time. Gently, though, not painfully. It is as if someone is injecting me with a powerful medicine that makes my entire body feel as though it is magnetized. I have never felt this for three consecutive days before. I have had glimpses of this experience during my meditation practices, but in my twenty years of meditating, it's never happened like this: continuously. I feel immersed in love and bliss! I find myself unable to sleep from the wonder of it all. I just want to thank the Universe and pray for my sister, brother-in-law and for the world. I feel I can't do anything else! Spontaneously I pray with love and gratitude yet, simultaneously, I hear this annoying, inner continuous message: 'Nalanie, prepare yourself. Prepare yourself.' I assume the message is to prepare me for when I return to New Jersey, to carry on supporting my sister through her husband's illness.

I had not been back to the Ashram for five years. After my Master's exit from our world there was an atmosphere of fear and uncertainty that engulfed the Ashram. This was hard for me, as the Ashram had always been my refuge, so I avoided going. However, with this visit, I can feel a shift. Love is re-emerging; there are changes in the energy field and lightness in the air! Everyone is healing after his passing! I finally truly understand how attachment to the physical body can stop our progress, our spiritual progress, in life. Things can stay stagnant for a long time if one does not embrace the separation from our body as the most natural thing in the world. The Ashram community has begun to accept the loss of the Master and is renewed by the knowledge that the teachings remain with them constantly. The atmosphere is charged with holy vibrations. And I am absorbed in peace.

After three days of quiet bliss, I return to New Jersey. I see that both Kantu and her husband are much more peaceful. The block and denial that they had in their hearts is dissipating. They had needed time alone to move past some of their fears. I also notice a deterioration in Vijay's physical health. His energy level is really low. He can hardly walk and he feels dizzy most of the time. He is losing weight rapidly.

Upon departing to my home in Spain, my sister embraces me and thanks me. My brother-in-law invites me to come more often. I leave with both joyful optimism hoping for the best, and a heart full of pain.

I feel excited by the fact that I am now going home to see my family and husband. I had missed him so much, especially after witnessing what happened between my sister and Vijay. I want to go back and just love him and thank him and make use of each moment. I am excited to see my daughter and three granddaughters. My third granddaughter, Talia, has special needs and she is only a year old. We later learn she suffers with mitochondrial disease and can hardly move. I think about how we have had a tough year, and how my daughter has served so unconditionally. I'll never forget what my daughter said to me. She said, "Mom, please don't ever worry about me. God sent me an angel in the form of Talia and my job is to make sure that she has the most perfect life possible in her broken body. And I don't mind cancelling all of my dance classes and activities, rearranging my life, because God has sent me an angel." I remember how later that night, I sobbed with joy that I, myself, also had an angel as a daughter. She had learned the true spirit of unconditional love and selfless service. I wondered if I could ever be like her.

I am also worried about my brother Maj who lives in England and was recently diagnosed with stage three throat cancer. Shanky and I had decided we would visit him in Birmingham at the end of the month. They are so close and Shanky was devastated when he heard of Maj's cancer. Yes, we could go to the UK and support my brother and shower him with love.

With these thoughts of excitement, I land at Malaga airport feeling jetlagged, as I had not slept on the flight. I walk out of the airport and am surprised to see my daughter with Talia in her arms, waiting for me.

I ask her, "Shani, what are you doing here? Where is Dad?"

"Mom, I need to speak with you. Dad has not stopped coughing. That is why he made his phone conversations with you very short. He didn't want you to worry. He is really sick and lost a lot of weight."

I look at her, confused. "But I've only been gone for twelve days."

"Twelve days, twelve kilos. He looks grey, and when he said he was planning to pick you up from the airport I got scared. I didn't know how he could make the one-hour drive to the airport alone. I just made up the excuse that I was tired of being home with housework and I wanted Talia to spend some time with him, and that I wanted to see you, that I've missed you so much."

We walk towards the car and I try to hide the shock I feel as I approach him. How is this possible? What has happened? It has only been twelve days! As he drives us home, the coughing is non-stop, almost as if he is gagging, and he is in so much pain with every cough.

I look to my left and say, "Darling when we get home we will pack some suitcases. I'm taking you to the hospital."

"No", he says, "tomorrow is Tara's birthday (our eldest granddaughter) and I promised her I would be there."

Firmly I reply, "Tara will have many birthdays. She won't mind if we miss this one."

We arrive home and I watch him sit on the bed while I pack. He is crouched with his hands on his abdomen in pain. I just want to cry, but I don't. I feel numb. I call our friend Peter Borge.

"Peter, the steroids have not helped. Something is very wrong. I want to take him to the hospital. What do you suggest?"

"Yes, take him to the hospital immediately."

We drive to the hospital where a room is instantly organized and Shanky is sent away for an X-ray. The radiologist looks at the results of my husband's X-ray. She shakes her head but when I ask, she doesn't tell me what's wrong.

"It's not my job to tell you. The doctor will speak with you shortly."

That awful dread, the *awful* dark feeling rises in my heart again. I smile, thank her, hug my husband and take him to the next room to see the oncologist, who tells us they need to do a biopsy immediately. The results will follow in a week's time.

I ask the oncologist, "Please, what can you do to stop this horrible cough?"

"I'll try to give him something. It may not stop, but the *Codeine* will still it a little and help him to sleep."

The next day comes and my husband has had his biopsy. The gastroenterologist looks at me and gives me the biggest hug ever. I know what I don't want to know.

He says with a consoling voice: "Just wait for the biopsy and the results".

I take my husband home and the cough is a little better but still has not stopped. The drugs seem to work and he sleeps at night, but I can't. I put my hand on his chest and repeat the *Mahamrityunjaya mantra**, a sacred prayer in Sanskrit for healing and self-realization. The whole night, it just keeps on going through my head.

The rest of the week feels blurry. My daughter calls me to support me, but she has her hands full with three young children, one with special needs. I am more worried about her and how she will cope. But when I look at her, I see it in her eyes that she knows. She is a wise girl. Even with the three little ones she tries to see her Dad as much as possible.

After what seems the longest week ever, we are back at the hospital to see the oncologist. He looks at my husband and I, and says, "I'm so sorry. It's stage four and it's completely metastasized. I don't know if we can help you, however there *is* one chance. There is a new chemo that is out and very strong. I'd like to give it a chance."

Shanky says, "Give us a time frame".

"You can live about six weeks without chemo and with chemo, maybe one year. But one never knows, as we have had exceptions where people get better. I know of one case. And Shanky, you are young and a strong man, you could be the next one."

My husband replies, "I would like that year".

Internally, I am screaming. This can't be real! This can't be real! This is so... surreal! He was fine just twenty days ago and now stage four cancer? He is going to die? Thirty-four years together? Once he has finally retired and started to enjoy a little bit of his life? This isn't right. Please, please Universe, tell me this is a bad dream. First Vijay, and then my brother Maj, and now Shanky. What on earth is happening?

The doctor suggests we get to the hospital to start the first treatment immediately, as nothing but the chemo will stop the coughing at this point. The tumour is blocking one of the nerves and this is the reason for the persistent cough.

* See appendix A

We leave the doctor's office and I break down in tears. I sob and sob and I say, "I'm so sorry, darling. I'm so sorry, darling. I'm so sorry, darling."

And he says, "Don't say anything to the kids."

"I *have* to tell our children. We've never lied to them, and I will *never* lie to them."

I call my daughter first. She says, "Oh Mom, I'm so sorry. Should I come and see you now?"

"Just wait. I'm going to call Shaman (my son, who had left Spain just two months prior to live in Hong Kong with his wife and start his own business). He will never forgive me if I don't tell him."

I call Shaman. I can't stop crying. I feel so awful but I really can't hold it. "Shaman, Dad has stage four cancer and we're starting chemo tomorrow."

"Mom, I'm coming."

"No, wait. You've just started your life. I'll tell you when I need you. I'll call you when I need you. Sort your life out. You're going through the newness of starting your own business and that's not easy."

"Mom, I really don't care. I'm coming and flying out tomorrow."

"What about your wife and baby?"

"They will understand."

His baby is only five months old. Indira is her name.

The doctor books us into a room. I ask him, "Please doctor, can we go home for a while? We need a couple of hours just to collect our thoughts and get some clothes."

He says, "No problem. Come back in 2 or 3 hours."

When my husband gets in the car and starts the ignition, I find myself suddenly getting angry - really angry - angry at him. I hear my mind thinking, 'I wish you had listened to me when I told you not to smoke so much.'

He had given up for eight years but prior to that he smoked 40 to 60 cigarettes a day. I wish he had listened to me when I told him not to eat so much white bread and meat. I remember the joke he shared in front of my yoga friends and students: "My wife and I make a perfect couple. I eat all the meat and she eats all the veg, and guess what, she is a really cheap date to take out!" All these thoughts are running through my mind and just as I am about to express my anger, my yogic practices of so many years take over. I hear my Master's voice, 'your husband has just been told that he might leave this earth and you are thinking about your anger? Where is the compassion in you? Have you forgotten everything you've learned? Serve, love, give, and now it's suddenly about *you?'* So I swallow the anger and instead say to him, "Darling, I'm so, so, so sorry. We will go through this together. There is no one or nothing to blame. This is no one's fault. It is as it is."

He is crying at this point. Sobbing and sobbing, and I just hold him. He says, "I'm sorry."

"Why are you sorry? You are the one that is suffering."

"I am sorry I'm hurting you."

"Remember, it is as it is."

And throughout the last weeks of our life together, every time our emotions got too hard for us to understand and digest, we would just look at each other and say, "it is as it is", and that helped us through.

Chapter 2
Hospital and Reminiscences

My daughter and I were relieved when Shaman arrived two days later. He possesses the same charisma as his Dad, the same aura. When you are around them you just feel safe and secure. When he hugged me, a wave of peace flooded my body. I sensed he would take care of all of the logistics because, at that moment, I just had too much to cope with. Shani was thrilled to see her brother. They were always very close and shared a special bond. She wanted to help more but couldn't with the three girls, Tara aged 8, Natasha aged 6 and Talia just 1 year old and struggling. I knew she was frustrated, as she wanted to be with us all the time. Saying that, she practically *was* with us all the time! I think back and I don't know how she and her husband, Andrew, managed it.

Shanky was touched to see his children being so supportive. His face broke into a huge smile whenever either of them walked into the room. We both didn't want their lives to be disturbed and disrupted but at the same time we were grateful for their presence. As for me, I don't think I had ever felt so vulnerable but having them by our side made me feel strong again.

We were very blessed to be in a hospital with rooms facing the seaside in Marbella. When we checked into the room and looked out of the window, we actually felt really optimistic. Looking at the clear, November blue sky, the waves glittering as if there were a thousand diamonds on them gave Shanky and I hope. Hope that he would survive this wretched disease. Hope that there would be a better tomorrow for us.

He looked at me and said, "Huns (short for 'honey', that's what he always called me) look out at that beautiful view and just visualize that we are on a cruise."

I smiled and remembered the cruise we had enjoyed a year prior. Just the two of us. It was as if we were on our honeymoon again. We had such a great time and never argued once! I laugh now to think of it. We often argued about silly things, as our belief systems were quite different. He always felt I was a bit bohemian and 'kooky', always talking about the ethereal world and the benefits of meditation and Yoga. And yet, on that cruise we spoke about our differences and realized how much we had both grown in accepting each other's ways. He even said he would travel with me more and help me with my work. I was so very excited when he said that, as I felt he finally understood me, and why I did what I did. I wanted so earnestly, from the bottom of my heart, to make a difference. To make our world a kinder place to be in. To give others hope! I felt so blessed having the family I had, and I realized there were so many that needed my help, those from broken homes and traumatic backgrounds. This I felt deeply was my *svadharma* (God given duty).

"You know, you gave me the best two occasions in my life besides the kids," he said.

"I did?"

"Yes. The cruise last year and the surprise party you threw for me on my 60th birthday".

It was a wonderful 60th birthday. He was truly amazed, as he had no idea that we were planning it. My daughter-in-law, Hersha who was six months pregnant at the time, and Shaman had helped with all the preparations and organization. We invited sixty friends that he and I were close to and, of course, our grandchildren, Tara and Natasha. We had managed to get a baby sitter for Talia. We commissioned a singing duo called 'The Valerga Brothers' to play his favourite songs. And during the evening Shanky sang the song he had written for me many years earlier, called 'The Other Side'. I asked him, at the time he had composed it, why the lyrics were about dying when he was petrified of dying and hated when I brought up the subject of death. His answer then was that he did not know why. He said the words and music just came to him.

Now I realize that the Soul knows certain phenomena in advance, before the mind and body does. Throughout my years of counselling I ascertained that many people received indications about their 'departure time' from this life but just did not know how to decipher the signs.

I became conscious of the fact that I was reminiscing and brought myself back to the moment. I started unpacking and brought out pyjamas for him to get into. I also unpacked my clothes, as I had decided to stay with him at the hospital for whatever time it took.

After a while, the oncologist walked in. He looked uncomfortable. My heart went out to him. What a job! We both looked at him and my husband blurted out, "Doctor, I want the truth. Please do not mince your words. I prefer to know if the chemo is really worth trying. My wife is not keen on it but I feel if it gives me a chance I want it."

"Mr Chellaram, your case is extremely serious. You are young, strong and I feel you must give it a try. It will not cure you but will give you at least a year more of life and in a year anything can happen."

"Then, doctor, I will. We can start straight away. This cough is driving me insane and every time I move my ribs hurt and my body is in so much pain."

My heart ached to hear he was in perpetual pain. 'You must stay strong, Nalanie. Hold on to your Guru, hold on to the Divine Presence', I told myself.

"We will start right away. The nurse will come around and prepare you for the intravenous chemo. It will be quite strong and you may feel weak, dizzy and nauseous. You will also lose your hair."

Shanky broke into a laugh and said, "Doctor, I am already nearly totally bald so there is not much to lose, just some off the sides!" That eased the tension that was building up in the atmosphere. I just felt total admiration for my husband and how he managed to lighten things up.

After the chemo was done, Shanky went into a deep sleep. The doctor had prescribed a strong sleeping pill. My daughter, her husband and the grandchildren came in after school hours to see how Shanky was doing. I felt numb.

After the children left, a feeling of dread washed over me. My whole marriage flashed in front of me. All the things we had been through! I married Shanky so young. I was only 20 and we were madly in love. We were living in Hong Kong, where I was born, and immediately after our marriage we moved to Gibraltar because his family's retail business there was in dire straits and run by his elderly uncle who refused to move with the times. Being the eldest son, Shanky felt it was his duty to sort the problem out. On returning to Hong Kong after our honeymoon, I was shocked by the change of attitude of my mother-in-law towards me. I was suddenly her property and had to get her permission every time I wanted to go out! This to me was unacceptable. I did really get to love her whilst Shanky and I were engaged but I could not condone this old Indian way of thinking and archaic behaviour! To say the least, my relationship with my mother-in-law deteriorated rapidly and that caused Shanky a lot of pain. And her. And me.

Indian traditions just did not make sense to me and still don't! For an Indian girl to stand her ground in their eyes was disrespectful and uneducated behaviour. And because I didn't conform, I was labelled as the 'bad daughter-in-law'. In my mind it was just so weird, as I always thought that all I wanted to be was kind and good and loving to everyone, and here I was filled with anger! So, when life gave us the option to move to Gibraltar we thought that distance would be a great healer and things would resolve themselves. It did finally but only after many, many years and through much aggression, pain and accusations. It was only because of my spiritual journey that I could forgive and let go and ask my mother-in-law to forgive me. I was truly sorry I was not the daughter-in-law she wanted but not sorry for what I believed in.

The first few years were full of hardship. The family business had no money and we had to work extremely hard to keep it afloat. If it wasn't for having my children, I truly believe that I may have done something quite horrible. I literally felt like Cinderella! My family home in Hong Kong was luxurious, comfortable and loving. In Gibraltar I walked into a dark, dirty grey home full of gloom. Shanky's uncle was always complaining and no matter how hard I tried to clean and cook for him, nothing was ever good enough. He used to insult me just because my family was wealthy. He was also unbelievably miserly and would not allow me to have a washing machine, and heaven help me if I left the cooker on too long or ran the hot water! The situation between Shanky's uncle and I became so unbearable that one day in the kitchen I offered him a large knife and told him he could kill me if he wanted to, as I'd had enough!

My poor husband just couldn't believe that he had taken me out of the lap of luxury and a life of ease into such hardship and comparative squalor. He told me to go back to Hong Kong till he could make some money. I answered, "I married you for better or worse, and this is the worse! But it will pass".

And pass it did, as everything in life does. I learnt to adapt, adjust and accommodate. No, it wasn't easy. I cried a lot those first years until I realized that I was only hurting myself and my family. Then the tears dried up. I worked hard in the shop. Raising my children brought me great joy, and I even started a dance school. I loved teaching dance and to my surprise there were no contemporary dance schools in Gibraltar at that time, so we immediately became extremely popular and grew to have over 150 pupils! The dance school went brilliantly and was so successful until I eventually damaged my knees from all the hours of working in the shop, working in the home and teaching dance. It was simply too much for my body and that is when I learnt, 'what you over-use, you lose. What you don't use, you also lose.'

The great change in my life happened when, at 33 years of age, I suddenly realized that despite all I had been doing I had become somewhat disappointed with life. Business had picked up and we finally had some money behind us so we were able to send our children to boarding school in England. Gibraltar was (and still is) a small place - three and a half square miles - and we wanted them to be more 'international' in their outlook. The astonishing thing was they actually wanted to go abroad to experience new things. Both of them were hard workers and by nature loved challenges. However, for me, their leaving felt as though the reason for my being had suddenly disappeared. In addition, and coincidentally, my doctor had informed me that I could no longer dance otherwise I would permanently destroy my knees.

Kids gone. No more dancing. Working in a business I never chose. And, on top of all that, witnessing the constant disputes between my in-law family! What was life all about? I never expected a bed of roses, but I never expected so much anguish either!

It was at this point in my life that everything turned around. One afternoon I refused to go to work and just stayed home and cried and cried. I shouted at the empty room, 'if there is a God, show your face, or

I will never be good again!' I now laugh just to think of it because, in retrospect, as a rebel back then I was never really good in the first place!

The following day I received a call from Swami Satchidananda. I had not heard from him since Shanky and I married. Why was he calling?

"Nalanie", he said, "I am going to Zinal in Switzerland to attend a Peace Conference, may I come and see you after that?"

"Of course, Swamiji", I answered.

"I will get my secretary, Prem Anjali, to contact you to sort out all the details."

Swamiji was our family Guru and I had known him since I was five years of age. He visited Hong Kong regularly at my father's invitation, attended family weddings, taught us Yoga, etc. All our family loved him. He reminded us of how we imagined Moses would look. He was also somewhat of a celebrity, as it was Swami Satchidananda who gave the opening address at the famous 'Woodstock Music & Arts Fair' back in 1969, and who was one of the leading lights who brought Yoga to the west.

I panicked. What do I do with Swamiji? Should I organize a talk? Where would he stay? We lived in a small apartment with one bathroom. Should I book him a hotel? How do we pay for it all? We barely had enough to send the kids to school and pay all our bills!

'When the student is ready, the teacher appears,' is an age old saying. And for me he did appear! Everything worked like clockwork. Everything flowed. Whatever I needed was brought to me. We had a wealthy client who loved our family, and she and her husband insisted Swamiji stayed with them in their huge villa in the South of Spain, and Shanky and I could also stay. In addition, she employed an Indian chef for the entire time of Swamiji's visit! Shanky designed a poster for the talk we asked Swamiji to give, which we advertised in the local paper. Full page and all for free! How did that happen? I learnt later that when you are around a great Soul, he subliminally weaves his magic to make everything easier for his host or hostess if what they organize is coming from a place of love.

The week that Swamiji was with us changed all our lives. Like a mist of pure white light, I felt his compassion and love pour over all of us. We felt something mystical and exhilarating embrace us. I felt as if I was cocooned in a cloud that was warm and safe. The spirit within me was awakened and I felt this inexplicable joy, the joy I had thought was lost forever.

The day Swamiji was leaving, I asked him if he would be my Guru. I was fearful that the bubble of peace I experienced would burst open and leave me devastated after his departure.

"Swamiji, my life can never be the same again, I cannot go back to my old way of thinking. What can I do, Swamiji?"

He smiled the most gentle of smiles and said, "Purify your mind. Think good thoughts. Love where you are. Learn to accept everything as part of the Divine Cosmic plan. Stop complaining. Meditate. When you are ready, God will use you."

"But I don't know how to meditate!"

"You do Nalanie, you have read many books about it and now you just need to practise."

That was the beginning of my true spiritual journey. I did meditate every day and witnessed the nonsensical chatter that existed in the field of my thoughts. My God, I had not realized what a mess of a mind I had! As soon as I sat down to meditate all the negative emotional garbage surfaced. I was shocked to witness the state of my mind. 'My God,' I said to myself 'how can I ever complain about anybody else when I must be the worst person I know?' I sincerely prayed for guidance and worked so hard to change those mental viruses into blessed thoughts. I watched myself every time I complained or started to blame someone else for something that was disturbing me. I later found out from the *Yoga Sutras of Sri Patanjali* that this practice had a name. It is called *Pratipaksha Bhavana.*

"When disturbed by negative thoughts, opposite, positive ones should be thought of."

(Yoga Sutras of Sri Patanjali, Book 2, Sutra 32)

This powerful practice, along with my mantra was and remains my saving grace. I truly am glad for all the years of practising, as it sustained me through this dark period.

I watched Shanky sleep and I prayed. I prayed with all my heart, all my soul:

'Dear, dear Divine Creator, please give me the strength to accept the things I cannot change but if you can, if it is at all possible, please make him well. And if not, please give him peace. If you are listening, please do not let him suffer! Please make me kind and strong so I can take care of him in the best way possible. And give me the grace not to be so fearful. Please guide us on this journey, which at the moment is our worst nightmare. I know you are with me but please don't allow my pride and selfishness to get in the way.'

"Huns, are you awake?"

"Yes, why? Can you hear me thinking?"

"Yes, I can."

I walked over to the hospital bed and snuggled in next to him. We held each other tightly. Both of us felt as if a bombshell had hit us. I started to repeat my mantra out loud and we both fell asleep praying for an easier tomorrow.

Shaman arrived early the next morning so that I could go down to the hospital coffee shop and have a nice cup of coffee. How I looked forward to the smell of the hot buttered toast and delicious coffee. It was medicine for my soul, fuel for my body.

I left the two men to discuss the finances. Money to me was an instrument to be used to serve and for that it was necessary. However, Shanky always thought differently. He always felt we never had enough and that caused a strain throughout our married life. I must admit though, in the earlier years, I was exactly the same. Now, more than ever, I was so grateful that we had money in the bank so we could look after him. I was grateful that we had medical insurance and he could stay in this comfortable hospital with these kind doctors.

For my darling son, I was filled with gratitude. He talked to lawyers, organized paperwork for the insurers, and so on. My job was then only to look after my beloved husband.

The second night after the chemo, Shanky woke me up at 3am.

"Huns, I would like you to read this email I have written to my brother."

'What!' I thought. *'Now, at 3 am?'*

Reluctantly, I got up from the sofa bed and went to his computer. Tears streamed from my eyes. Shanky and his brother never got along. I felt his younger brother was always envious of Shanky and as a result created a lot of problems for us during our married life. He had lied about Shanky and spread horrible rumours about his character. The email my husband wrote was one asking for forgiveness and offering his forgiveness. To allow bygones to be bygones. Shanky requested his brother to please look after their parents and sisters in the event he would not make it through this illness.

"It's beautiful, Darling," I said. "It's the height of compassion and forgiveness. I feel so proud of your big, kind, heart. After all he had done to you, you are able to let it all go. I thought I was the Yogi, but you truly are the one, not me."

"I love you, Huns. I am so sorry I never said it enough during our marriage and I promise you I will tell you how much I care every day from now on."

"Don't make me cry! I finally learnt to live without you saying it because I understood your actions were louder than words! You have always shown your love in so many ways. I know I took a long time to realize that."

For years I had begged him to just say those words until a time came when I really did not need to hear them. I had realized that the Divine had brought us together for him to teach me not to be so needy and pathetic. I was quite proud of the fact that I had indeed become stronger. Standing there, listening to him, reading the letter, I clearly saw all those lessons we had come to learn from each other. There was never any wrong or right. Not any better or worse, but a joining of two souls who voluntarily decided to come together to bring out the best in each other. To learn to accept our differences, to learn that love truly conquered all. All those arguments we had, all those tears meant that our egos were just being rubbed and scrubbed! Our life together flashed through my brain and the only thing that seemed really important now was that he got better. All I felt was this immense love and gratitude for our time together.

Chapter 3
The Roller Coaster Ride Begins

'Like two golden birds perched on the selfsame tree, intimate friends, the ego and the Self dwell in the same body. The former eats the sweet and sour fruits of the tree of life while the latter looks on in detachment'

(Mundaka Upanishad, Part 3, Verse 1)

In the days that followed I constantly had the feeling of being in a dream. Nothing seemed real. I recall feeling that I was walking on a tightrope, constantly trying to keep my balance by focusing on each moment. Shanky's breathing had become worse and now he needed oxygen constantly. One good thing though, that racking, nagging cough had finally abated.

Shaman, what a saviour! He talked with his Dad and organized all the paperwork. They talked about wills, about what would happen to me if Shanky left. Accounts, bank accounts - all the things I disliked tremendously. Throughout our married life, I allowed Shanky to handle all our finances. Whatever I received from the sale of my home or from my father, I handed to him. I really never was interested. All I ever wanted was to always have enough to pay my bills, look after my children, grandchildren and to be free. Suddenly, everything seemed daunting. The prospect of being in charge of finances felt like a rope around my neck. At the same time, I also felt a release, as I would not have to answer to anybody about what I spent. Shanky was constantly concerned for my future but I knew deep in my heart that I was always looked after. The two birds existed within me and I was fluctuating constantly from being the observer of circumstances to being the actress in the play. A vibrant energy awoke from deep within my soul, a power that I did not know I had. Well, was it really mine?

I was determined to make my husband as comfortable as possible. I must say this truly was very selfish of me, as I could not bear to watch him suffer.

One day, I asked the doctor if I could take my husband home where I knew he would be more comfortable. What was the point of being in hospital if there was nothing they could do till the next chemo treatment, which was to be in the next couple of weeks? The doctor said that it would be hard on us but my son and I were determined to nurse Shanky and felt we could do it. However, we needed to have a visiting doctor to monitor him. We also needed to buy an oxygen machine for the home, which Shaman organized and had ready at home in no time. When the mind accepts the challenges, life just flows. I couldn't believe our blessings when our friend Michele called us and told us that her daughter Lulu was a palliative care doctor who worked for a charitable organization. How did she know? I grabbed the opportunity and Lulu arrived at the hospital that afternoon to check with the oncologist the list of drugs and care Shanky needed at home. When we first saw Lulu, she looked like a little girl. My husband asked me how on earth we could put his life in her hands. But, after talking to her and watching her go about things with total comprehension and authority, he learnt to accept her and went on to develop a deep friendship with her.

The journey home was tough. The ambulance arrived and we realized that Shanky had lost the strength in his legs. It was difficult to dress him but I pretended it was the easiest thing in the world. Shani and Shaman looked at me, questioning with their eyes, *'Mom, can we really do this?'*

Oh, but was it worth it! To see the smile on Shanky's face when we arrived home gave us all so much joy. We knew we had done the right thing. The only problem was the bed. I needed to buy a hospital bed, as it was impossible to make him comfortable just by propping up the pillows, so Shaman and I rushed out to buy the bed whilst Shani looked after her father.

Whenever I left Shanky to either purchase medications or to get household conveniences, it always felt that everything took so long. It was hard to leave him and when I took longer than expected, he would get agitated and ask for me continuously. My soul knew time was short and I wanted to spend every waking moment with him.

"Mom," Shaman said. "I need to talk with you. None of us know what is going to happen here. I will not leave Dad and you to go back to Hong

Kong. However, I want my wife and baby to come and be here with us. We don't know how long this will take."

"Shaman, how will we manage with a baby, with all that is going on already?"

"Mom, trust me. Hersha is so capable and really she will look after Indira. You really do not have to take it upon yourself."

My nature was always to look after everyone. I had this motherly instinct that whoever walked into my home had to be treated to the best of my ability. Suddenly this feeling was overwhelming. I felt I couldn't cope with another thing. I looked at my son, his face pleading with me to understand. And he was right. It was not correct for him to be away from his family indefinitely.

"Yes, Shaman Ok. Ask her to come. We will all manage and work together."

He called her immediately and she arrived with beautiful Indira a few days later. And having her there was a great gift.

We were living in a beautiful ground floor apartment on top of a hill with a glorious view of the sea and Gibraltar in the distance. We had three bedrooms and three bathrooms so there was space for the family to stay.

Every morning around six, Shanky would be up and Shaman, hearing us, would rush into the room, help me wash Shanky and take him with the oxygen tank to the sitting room where we would spend the day watching movies and videos. We tried to make life as normal as possible. Shani and Shaman began researching other avenues, other forms of treatments for healing cancer. They looked at all kinds of alternatives and found a centre not far away in Malaga that specialized in different types of natural treatments. However, Shanky was not open to these alternatives and was not convinced at all.

At this time, he was hardly eating. We all decided we would just give him what he desired. And of all things, he wanted frozen grapes to chew on and a bottle of beer every evening. This made him joyful and at those moments in the dusk light we would have the deepest of conversations.

"Darling, are you scared?" I asked one evening whilst the children were out buying take away food.

"I am not scared," he answered. "I don't want to suffer like this. I feel so useless and I feel awful that everyone has to stop their lives for me."

"Darling, don't you realize it is such an honour to look after you?"

"That kind of honour I don't need in my life!"

"Do you think about dying? Are you afraid of dying? You always hated the subject. Do you want to tell me how you feel?" It was the hardest question I ever had to ask my husband, yet I had asked this question so many times to other people with such ease.

"You know, Huns, I thought I would be a lot worse. I wish I could live just another six months. I would do so much more for you. I am only worried about leaving you alone. How will you cope? You must learn to drive properly. Sell the old cars and buy yourself a new one. You will need to move from here. It's too isolated in the winter."

"Darling, please don't worry about me. You know me. I can be really independent when I want to be. Let's just focus on getting you better. Let's not give up hope until there really is no hope. The doctor said you are strong and who knows, you could recover! What I want to know is, how do you feel about soul, spirit?"

"I trust you. I know you will guide me when the time comes. I know that if anyone can heal me spiritually it will be you. Please tell all your Yogi friends to stop offering me healing, as I really do not have faith in any of them. They are good people, but it just doesn't click with me."

I was shocked to hear this. He often told me in the past that he thought all I was doing was just a waste of time. And now suddenly he had complete faith in me! Tears filled my eyes and rolled down my cheeks.

"Please Huns, don't cry. I really cannot bear to see you sad." He really meant that, for the next day he told Lulu that he found it hard to hear me crying during the nights, and she advised me to stop crying in front of him.   So, I did.   I tried to make him smile by holding his face in the palms of my hands and telling him I loved him so much.   I started to dress up every morning for him.   I thought that if I would look pretty, he would not want to leave me.   Stupid, childish thoughts.   But he did notice and said he loved the way I dressed for him every day.

As the days went by, his body became thinner and thinner.   I felt as if someone had strangled my heart with a rope.   In my mind, I prayed relentlessly.   I hardly slept at all.   Maybe a couple of hours a night.   I watched him vigilantly, observing his breath.   My meditation practice sustained me.   My thoughts kept fluctuating from the present to the past to the future.   So many thoughts, so many realizations flooding my mind.   And yet, at the same time, there was stillness, a voice telling me again and again, *'It is as it is.   All is as it should be.'*

Before we knew it, it was time to take him back to the hospital for the second chemo.   Two days prior, he had started to gain some strength again and his appetite was better.   He actually asked for bowls of fruit. The children and I were much enthused by this.   Maybe the chemo was working.   Miracles happen!

I did not want him to start the second treatment.   Not yet.   I wanted him to wait while we continued our research.   I told him so but he answered that he wanted the chemo, that he liked and trusted his doctor, and he was finally beginning to have a little more energy.   He felt it was his only chance.

At this point, he became quite chatty and positive.   He started telling his old jokes again, which I was tired of but suddenly, under those circumstances, hearing them gave me such pleasure and I just laughed out loud!   That made him really happy!

Why is it that we human beings take things for granted and only start appreciating them when they are suddenly going to be taken away from us?   This was a big lesson for me.

Shanky never complained and bore whatever pain he had quietly.   That just made me love him more.

The ambulance arrived and we trudged back to the hospital. This time there was no room with a sea view. I asked the nurse to make sure that if any became available, she would give us first priority.

"Darling, are you sure you want to go ahead with this?"

"Yes Huns, I have to try. Please understand."

He was never the same after that chemo. He started to experience many side effects. First, he started getting seizures, which initially freaked me out. I remember so clearly chatting with him when his eyes suddenly rolled up and it looked as though he was having an epileptic fit. I shouted out for the nurse and when she entered the room, the seizure stopped. Shanky looked at me blankly and asked, "What happened? Why are you all around me?" I explained and told him not to worry. Ha! How was that even possible?

That night I looked out of the window and watched the streetlights and people walking on the streets. I looked up at the night sky and at the beautiful array of stars. Stunning. Pleasure and pain, life and death. Love and the dance of life. All a dream. Where did the years go? Where was God? Where is God? Everywhere but nowhere to be seen. Where was I? Who am I?

I turned to look at my husband's troubled sleep and just sighed. I realized that I don't know anything at all. How many before me have gone through this? How do they cope without the spiritual teachings? It must be torture for them if this is what all life leads to and they have no belief in the soul. I spent the night repeating my mantra, as sleep again evaded me.

The next morning was not better. Shaman came in early so that I could have a shower and a break. I constantly needed to get out of the hospital and just walk by the beach. It was essential that I had quiet time to clear the cobwebs in my brain. When I got back from my walk, Shanky complained about a pain in his chest, so I asked the nurse to call the emergency doctor to see him. X-rays were taken and the result was that water was building up in his lungs. They needed to take him into the operating theatre immediately to release the water. The doctor explained that they would have to insert a tube in the side of his chest after the procedure and then they would have to leave it overnight to pump and drain the water out.

Shani rushed over and we all waited. Family. I was grateful for the comfort. We held hands. After a while, the doctor appeared and told us everything went well. Our children saw their Dad still groggy from anaesthesia and then rushed home to their families.

This was one of the worst nights for me. When Shanky came to, he was screaming in pain.

"Darling, this tube is awful! Please, please tell the doctor to remove it. I cannot bear it."

Ok, ok, Nalanie, get your thoughts together. It's eight in the evening. The doctor must have left. I called the nurse and she informed me that he was still in his office so I ran to the lift and got to his office as he was just about to leave.

"Doctor, please help! My husband is in agony. You know he has never complained and now he is screaming that he cannot bear the pain of the inserted tube. Doctor, please what can you do to alleviate his pain?"

"Nalanie, if we remove the tube the water will build up again."

"And if you leave it and remove it tomorrow, will it build up again or will it just stop happening?"

'There are no guarantees, but normally it does recur."

"What? So why make him go through this at all if it will just happen again?"

"It's procedure."

I screamed. "Procedure! What kind of procedure is it that causes more pain and in the end will bring no great results?"

"Nalanie, calm down. I will see him now before I leave."

I calmed down. "Thank you doctor. I am deeply grateful" I said, and gave him a huge hug.

He could hear my husband groan loudly as we entered the room.

He looked at me and at Shanky and said, "It must be touching one of his numerous tumours. I will remove the tube. I can see this is not helping the situation. Thankfully, it looks like much of the water has been drained away already."

When the tube was removed, Shanky burst out crying from the relief. The doctor gave him a strong painkiller and he soon fell asleep.

My phone rang. It was Peter, our good friend and doctor.

"How are things, Nalanie?"

That's when I just broke down outside the room, crouched on the hospital floor and sobbed.

Peter said patiently "It's alright, Nalanie. It's OK to cry."

"I'm sorry, Peter. It's just been the worst day ever. I couldn't bear to see his pain." I related what had happened to Shanky and he said I had done the right thing and it was lucky that the doctor in charge was so compassionate and obliging.

After we hung up, I thanked my lucky stars to have had the presence of mind to tell the doctor how I felt. I realized many people just allow doctors to do what they think is best and according to what is perceived to be the 'perfect procedure'. It's true that doctors generally do their best. I just realized it was more important to do what was best for the patient involved and not for what 'medicine required'. Wasn't medicine there to help alleviate suffering?

Another night of no sleep.

The following day the oncologist arrived and took Shanky for brain scans, x-rays, etc.

We got the results a few days later. No improvement. Cancer cells continue to metastasize.

"What next, doctor?" I asked.

"Well, we still need to try one more chemo in two weeks. The next one may help."

"So, what do we do in the meantime?"

"Well, he can stay here till then."

"For what, doctor? So that the nurses can poke him every few hours, take his blood and give him more pain? Is it going to make any difference?"

"No, not really. We can't know so soon."

I made up my mind. "Please allow us to take him home".

"It's a good idea if you can manage it," he replied. "Most people can't. It may give him encouragement and make his will to live stronger if he goes home."

"Thank you! Thank you!"

My husband's face broke into a huge smile. "Yes, doctor I want to go home and be around my children and grandchildren."

And there we went again, calling the ambulance, dressing him, struggling to maintain our positivity and praying the journey home would not be too difficult for him.

Chapter 4
"I Get By With Help From Family And Friends"

At the time just before my husband's diagnosis, I was running an Integral Yoga Centre across the border in Gibraltar. However, because I had moved over to Spain, I would only go into Gibraltar every week on a Wednesday. I would see clients and students all day and, in the evening, give a talk on the Science of Yoga. There were a group of students that I had trained and they served freely to keep the Centre open all week. The Centre was registered as a charity and everything ran on donations. I taught the students without charge and in return they offered their service to the Centre. No one was paid. All donations received were used for charitable purposes and given away almost as quickly as they came in!

Our mission was simply to spread peace and joy through understanding the power of the mind and learning how to harness our thoughts so that we could all live more loving and peaceful lives. We knew that body, mind and spirit are intrinsically linked so our job was to educate people about how to keep the body healthy and the mind pure so that spirit could enjoy the dance called *Life*. We were also involved with many charitable projects in different parts of the world. My life was full of meaning and I was extremely busy.

And it still is. I am quietly proud of the fact that the Integral Yoga Centre in Gibraltar is continuing with its mission.

Then as now, I love my work! I love the thrill of seeing individuals walk in feeling as though there was no hope and then leaving with enthusiasm, and inspiration to make themselves a better future. I love that people can help themselves by learning the Science. Yoga is not what most people think it is. They think it is only about exercising and getting into crazy contortions!

Yoga is a complete science on understanding *who* we are, why we are here and what medicine needs to be applied to achieve supreme peace whilst on earth. It's about transforming oneself rather than trying to change anyone else. It's about being in touch with the 'Self' in all of us.

> *'The Lord of Love is the one Self of all.*
> *He is detached work, spiritual wisdom,*
> *And immortality. Realize the Self.*
> *Hidden in the heart, and cut asunder*
> *The knot of ignorance here and now.*
> *Bright but hidden, the Self dwells in the heart.*
> *Everything that moves, breathes, opens and closes*
> *Lives in the Self. He is the source of Love*
> *And may be known through Love but not through thought.*
> *It is the goal of Life. Attain this goal!'*

> (Mundaka Upanishad Part 2, 1 & 2, from 'The Upanishads'
> Interpreted by Eknath Easwaran)

My personal mission is summed up by Master Sivananda:

'Serve, love, give, meditate, purify and realize! Do good, be good, be kind and compassionate.'

I travelled quite a lot worldwide, wherever I was invited to teach this Science or involved with Yoga retreats. We had a few charitable projects in Nepal, Sri Lanka and India, which I had to attend to. Shanky never liked the idea of me going to remote places and, although I always invited him to join me, he continuously refused till just a few months before he passed into the next dimension. It was on our last cruise that he told me he had decided he would travel with me and help me with the work. He came on a few trips to Portugal with me and absolutely loved it! I was thrilled he finally travelled with me! I was proud to show my husband off. He played the guitar and got everyone singing and all who met him, loved him.

When we moved to Spain, I also became quite involved with a group of people who desperately wanted to learn to meditate. One of them made available the basement of her home and we met there every week. We built up a strong *sangha* (a group of people who get together to discover the Truth). We started a charity in Spain too, and all proceeds went towards serving those in need. When Shanky was diagnosed, the first thing I did was to cancel all my programmes, appointments and lectures. I told all those concerned that it was my responsibility and honour to serve my husband. I reiterated that I had no idea when I would return and that they would all have to hold the fort and take care of all matters. And boy, did they do that - and more!

When Shanky and I returned home after the second chemo, *sangha* members would visit and bring dinner for me and for my family every evening so that I would not have to cook. Their kindness touched me so deeply. My family and I were extremely grateful for all the love we received from them. There is a saying, 'you are blessed if you can count your real friends on one hand'. Well, I was astounded to see that my two hands were not enough! The Gibraltar *sangha* sent messages of love and comfort constantly. Many of them came to visit at the hospital and at home. Their visits were such a highlight for my husband and our family. He would sit up to welcome them. One would not believe that he was sick at all if it weren't for the oxygen tubes. But, as soon as they left, he would collapse on the bed depleted of all energy.

My brother Maj, who was himself suffering with throat cancer, would call me daily from England. He loved Shanky and had helped him so many times when things were not going well for him in business. They had become close and we had promised to visit Maj but now, suddenly, Shanky was deteriorating rapidly.

Maj gave me great hope as I watched his positive attitude and his determination not to succumb to the disease. I am so grateful he is still here on this earth eleven years later and living a most beautiful, peaceful life with his angel of a partner, Sara.

My eldest sister Mira, really a Mom to me, called daily, too and her tenderness and love saw me through many dark days. My eldest brother David and his wife, Avisha, constantly kept in touch and offered together with Mira to come and help. But Christmas was approaching and I told them they needed to spend time with their families at home in Hong Kong. I had no time to really speak with Kantu in the States to tell her how much I had learnt from her and Vijay's case. My baby sister, Lavi was a stroke patient and living in Ghana, and the last thing I wanted was for her to worry. My other brother Kumar and his wife Manisha called regularly from Bangkok. We received messages of love from all over the world.

My husband's family called too, and Shanky was particularly happy to hear from his sisters, Lavina and Baghwanti. Shaman took over all the phone calls and filtered who could speak to me or to his Dad. There were days that I had no energy to answer people's questions. I needed every drop of strength to get through each day. It was particularly hard when people called to lecture and tell us how we should be looking after Shanky when they were miles away and had no clue what was happening.

A word of advice: When someone is sick, unless you are an expert in the field and fully aware of the facts, you should not offer any advice or lecture on the subject!

One particularly touching moment was when Les and Karen, two *sangha* members from Gibraltar, came all the way to see us and brought a video tape of all the 'Yogis' singing to Shanky, telling him how much they loved him and how they were waiting to see him better. It was such an uplifting video and he cried after watching it. Not because he was sad but because he was flabbergasted at the love that exuded from the video. I will never forget that moment when he said, "Huns, they really do love me!"

I answered, "Of course! I told you that so many times."

"But I thought they were only nice to me because of you!"

"What? Why wouldn't they love you? You are a good, kind man."

We just hugged each other and I could feel the peace in his heart.

My good friend Marina flew over from Barcelona to see him before she left for Nepal, where she was funding a nursery school project through her own charity, *Vida Util*. Another good friend, Ulla from Estoril in Portugal called with so much encouragement in her voice. Shanky's childhood friend Pico called every day. Other friends Julio, Paddy, Lilian, Michele and so many more! These calls, brimming with love and support, meant a lot to Shanky, myself and to our children.

Shani was amazingly strong. Shaman was desperate to find a cure for his Dad. He and Hersha relentlessly searched the Internet in the hope of finding that miracle cure. I was torn between waiting for that miracle and from knowing the reality of the situation. On the 8th December I prayed for a sign. I asked to be sent a huge, bright butterfly if he was not going to make it, and if I did not get that sign then 'Yay! Universe!' my husband would live!

It was the 9th December. Shanti, my lovely PA, brought a huge envelope for me. She said that someone we knew, Jennie who lived in England, had sent it to Gibraltar. I thought it must be a Christmas gift. I sat down at breakfast with Hersha and baby Indira and tore open the envelope. Out came a huge sequined, bright pink decorative butterfly. I screamed!

Hersha asked, "Moms, what's wrong?"

In that moment I couldn't speak. I later told her about my prayer and the sign I had asked the Universe to send me. I knew then. I knew Shanky was going to leave. My heart felt as if it had dropped to my stomach. It was time to prepare for the worst. But I could not let go of the thought that at the same time I should know that a miracle could still happen. The constant paradox of life. *Get yourself strong, girl. Prepare yourself. Prepare your husband and prepare the children.*

That afternoon, I spoke with Lulu, the palliative care doctor that came home daily. I asked her what she thought. She sighed and looked at me and said, "Nalanie, I know you are a positive person and believe in miracles. I have been looking after hundreds of cases like Shanky's and I am truly sorry to tell you that his case is too far gone. The cancer is all over. You should know that he told me the pain was becoming intolerable. We have to up his morphine slightly."

"How long, Lulu?"

"I cannot say how long. It depends on the patient. Some can live up to a year if they are not ready to let go, others leave in days. It's up to him and all your family."

Shaman was with me and he froze.

"No," he said. "I am sure we can find a cure. It's not fair! My Dad is too young. I promised him I would buy him a car and look after him and he has not given me the chance to do that. He cannot go yet."

"Shaman, over the years I have heard people promise cancer patients miracle cures. All I can tell you is, not one has worked when the cancer has metastasized all over." Lulu replied. "What I have seen is when one applies the power of the mind, it can change circumstances."

"It will be what it will be, Shaman," I said. "Nothing is in our hands. All that we can do is look after Dad to the best of our abilities and shower him with love. If there is anything you want to tell him, tell him now. If you need to thank him, thank him now. I have a great book called 'The Tibetan Book of Living and Dying'. Read the chapter on 'Helping the Dying'. It will help you."

"Mom, I find it hard to accept that."

"I know."

When we spoke with Shani, she looked knowingly at us and said she had already accepted the fact that her Dad would leave. I looked at her in admiration. She had so much to cope with. Talia was hardly eating and failing to thrive, and could not be left alone as she could not turn on her own. If she vomited, which she did often because she suffered from reflux, it would be extremely dangerous. Shanky and I made it a point to help Andrew and her as much as we could, taking the other two girls to and from school, and having them with us nearly every weekend. And now she received no help from us at all and I was concerned that with her father's illness it would just be too much for her. But no. She maintained great strength and fortitude. Hersha and Shani were like sisters. I was relieved they had each other.

Christmas was around the corner. We put up the Christmas tree with Shanky helping by passing us the decorations. It was both a sweet and bitter moment. *Would this be our last Christmas together?* As a family, we loved Christmas. Every Christmas Eve we would all have dinner together. We would share the cooking and spend the evening playing charades and having fun. Such a special time.

I had bought no presents! I needed to have time to shop.

"Sweetheart, would you mind if I went out for a couple of hours to the shopping centre with Shaman? We have no presents for anyone. You know I will be quick as I make fast decisions."

"Can I come with you?" he asked.

Shaman and I looked at each other and he said, "why not? We could take him in the wheelchair. Then we could take him out for a quick lunch and get him home."

The following day, we dressed him up, and with great difficulty placed him in the wheelchair and took him shopping. On the way there, Shanky said if it was at all possible, he would love to go to one of his favourite restaurants by the beach and that he fancied having lamb cutlets. We could not believe our ears! It was so difficult finding food that he would eat as he kept on saying everything tasted metallic. *'Yes'*, we thought, *'this is a good sign.'*

When we left home to go to the shopping Centre we took the oxygen machine in a bag and placed it next to him. However, as soon as we arrived, he started to look grey and tired. I rushed to do the shopping and when I returned to where he and Shaman were sitting, I could see Shanky was exhausted.

"Mom, I think we need to leave."

I cannot believe I actually felt irritated! I was so excited to be out, to see the lights and the Christmas decorations and the shops. I couldn't believe I had to rush home! I forgave myself later as I realized it was perfectly human to have these fleeting thoughts. I adjusted my attitude and we took him to the restaurant on our way home. We sat down to order the lamb chops for him. When the food arrived, he took one bite and said he could not eat it.

He looked at both of us with deep sadness and said, "I cannot even enjoy my favourite food."

And I heard him thinking, without spoken words. *'What's the point?'*

We rushed through our lunch and took him home.

Chapter 5
Final Days

I am trying to recollect what happened next and even now, after eleven years, thinking about it makes my mind feel fuzzy, full of cotton wool. I remember constantly trembling not because I was cold with the December wind, but trembling because I watched my husband become thinner and thinner with every passing day. I truly saw myself in the worst part of the movie called *Life*.

I knew that time was limited. The sparkly butterfly that was hung up in the corner of the room was reminding me of the storm that was to come. I asked Jennie a year later why she had sent me that cardboard sequined butterfly. She said she did not have a clue why. She explained that she was walking past the store and just thought 'I need to buy this for Nalanie. Does she like this kind of thing? Will she think I am mad?' And the next thing she knew, she bought it and posted it to me. That was two weeks before I had received it. Now that I know Jennie well, I know she has psychic abilities and just senses things. I told her the story and thanked her for giving me notice to prepare.

I did not give up hope but I could feel Shanky letting go. The pain was getting too much for him. He continuously complained that his mouth tasted of metal (the result of chemotherapy), his seizures became more frequent and I felt him slipping away.

One morning, as I wheeled him into the bathroom to wash him, I saw the tears roll down his face.

"Sweetheart, what's wrong? Have I hurt you?" I asked.

"Look at me, Huns. I look so old, thin and ugly. I don't recognize myself. I can't stand that I have to wear nappies. I can't stand that everyone has to look after me. I can't stand being confined to the bed and plugged in to an oxygen machine, and I cannot bear you and the kids hanging around looking after me all the time!"

"For me you will always be handsome!" I answered feebly, but I meant it.

"Don't be polite. I can see what this cancer is doing to me and I know that I don't have long. I really do not want to live if I have to live like this."

"Will you promise me one thing? Will you promise you will give me notice when you decide?"

"How much notice would you like?"

"Three days," I said.

"Okay, I will give you three days."

"But promise me also that you won't stop having hope? Prepare for the worst, which we have, but please, who knows, everything may change for the better tomorrow."

This is the dilemma that most people have to go through when they have a very sick partner. When does one let go and how long does one hold on for? Through this experience I learnt that this decision is really up to the ailing person. It is their call. When they are prepared, it is essential to be willing to help them leave their bodies in the most loving way. If they are not ready, it is important to prepare them towards the goal of acceptance. But in many cases this happens naturally as the patient finds it too hard and painful to be in the body.

I fought hard to hold back the tears. My heart broke for him and for me. I could see he really found it hard to look at himself in the mirror. That image will forever remain in my mind. My solace was my mantra. I repeated it over and over in my head so that I wouldn't fall into fear and depression. I fully embraced my role as his carer. The only thing I felt I needed to address was his wellbeing physically, mentally and spiritually. For that, I needed strength, courage and understanding of the process that we were going through. I found myself repeating a prayer that I asked my patients to echo when they couldn't deal with certain situations in their lives.

'Lord, grant me the serenity to accept the things I cannot change.
The courage to change the things I can.
And the wisdom to know the difference.'

It was the 15ʰ December and we had to take him to the hospital again for his third chemo. I was totally against it, but I had promised Shanky we would adhere to his wishes. Shaman and I had such a difficult time to get him dressed and into the ambulance. He was finding it so difficult to stand. When we got to the hospital, he was taken into a special room where they prepped him with all kinds of tests before they could start his chemo. As soon as all medical checks were over, Shanky fell asleep from exhaustion.

After a couple of hours, the doctor entered the room and stared at me.

"Doctor, before you give my husband the next chemo, please can I ask you to look at his legs and his body. His legs are thinner than mine and he has no strength. Will the chemo help him at all? After the last treatment, my husband's health deteriorated rapidly. He became more uncomfortable than ever. Please doctor, he has suffered so much. Please be truthful to me. If it were you, would you have the next treatment?"

The doctor uncovered the blanket and looked at my husband's frail body. He looked at me with such compassion. I could feel he was truly affected. He had gotten very close to Shanky. During our days in hospital, they would sit and enjoy a beer together in the evening before the doctor left for home. They would talk about the old days in Spain and tell each other jokes. I had scolded the doctor for allowing him to drink alcohol and the doctor chided me by saying that if it made him happy, that was the best medicine of all. I then continued to give Shanky a beer every evening at home and joined him by having a glass of wine. It did cheer him up no end!

"Nalanie, the test results are not good. The cancer has not abated but only become more aggressive. I sincerely thought the treatment would work, as he was such a strong man. I cannot make the decision for you but what I can tell you is that at this stage it will not help."

"Then doctor, I will take him home. But what should I do next? What can I do for him to make him comfortable?"

"I will prescribe a stronger dose of morphine and some other meds, and I'll talk to your palliative care doctor. Will you be able to deal with this? Would you need something to help you? I can prescribe some sleeping pills. I can see you need to rest. It will not be easy for you. I can see how much in love you both are."

"No doctor, I refuse to take anything. I have my yoga practices, which keep me strong. I have my family and my dear son and he is the best help in the world. His father feels so comfortable with him. Lulu is most capable and Shanky trusts her. Are you telling me there is nothing else we can do?"

He did not answer. He gave me a hug and wished me luck. I could see he felt defeated. I appreciated that he cared.

It was a hard trip home. Shaman and I were lost in our thoughts. We realized we had to be responsible for all Shanky's treatments now. The medical world could do no more. I was lost in thinking of methods I could use to make it easier for my darling husband, with all the spiritual knowledge I had. Help me Divine Consciousness! Help me Gurudeva!* Help me God, if you are there listening to me! The words 'prayers are strong, powerful thoughts' is a quote from Swami Satchidananda that resonated in my brain.

Home was a place for family for the next few days. Shani, Andrew and the three girls moved in. Indira was still a baby and needed a lot of loving care. My daughter-in-law Hersha was amazingly patient and so kind and helpful. My daughter was just a diamond, too! I was extremely grateful for their support. Shanky and I loved having them around but there were times we just wanted to be on our own. We used to put '*X Factor*' on the TV for him as he loved the show. But the last one was just too much for him. He felt it was just too noisy.

Shanky started to sleep more and more. Once when he awoke, I happened to be in the kitchen chatting with the kids and when I went back to the bedroom, he said, "Please don't ever leave me alone!" Oops, he was really upset!

*Gurudeva is a term of respect for one's Guru

After that, we never left him alone, there was always someone in the room with him. I found myself getting very weepy. I kept going to the bathroom to cry. I knew he was leaving. But, no! I told myself that I could not succumb to this feeling! I must not lose hope! But there before me, on the bed, was a skeleton of a man that was hardly my husband. Where did that powerful dynamic energy go? I knew then that I must be ready for the inevitable. I quickly applied some make up so that Shanky would not notice I had been crying.

Both my sister Mira and my sister-in-law Avisha called me on the 19th December to ask if they could fly from Hong Kong to be with me. I repeated that they should stay with their husbands and family and that it was too close to Christmas. But they both insisted they wanted to be with us and could leave Hong Kong on the 23rd December and arrive on Christmas Eve. Actually, I was thrilled to hear that, as I felt I would love their support. Immediately after they confirmed their travel plans, Shanky's two sisters said they too would fly over with Pico, Shanky's childhood friend, and they would all come on the same flight.

Where were they to stay? Shaman went to see the caretaker of our *Urbanization* (residential complex) who promptly told us of a three-bedroom apartment that was available for rent. We were relieved, as that would make visiting so much easier for everyone. Yet again the Universe was so obliging to make everything easy for us.

Early on Sunday morning, at around 5:30 am, Shanky said to me, "Huns, I am sorry. I really do not want to live like this. I cannot move. I am in terrible pain. Please, can I leave? Will you be alright?"

"Yes, sweetheart. If you cannot take it anymore, then let go. I am brave. I, too, do not want you to suffer anymore."

"Can you call my friends to come and see me today?"

"Yes, of course I can. Who would you like to see?"

"I would love to see Haresh and Anju, Peter and Sheila, Christian and Jane, Morris and Debbie, Michele and John, and Dennis and Barbara."

I asked Shaman to call them all and ask them if they were able to visit that afternoon for tea. They all agreed and arrived together. Prior to their arrival, Shanky spent most of the time asleep and could hardly move. A half an hour before they arrived, he shocked us all by sitting up and looking perky! He asked me if he looked decent enough. At that moment my heart skipped a beat, as I thought that maybe he would get better. Maybe seeing his friends would rekindle his enthusiasm for living! When they arrived and entered the bedroom he gave them a big smile and began talking to them candidly. He told them to make sure I bought a new car and learnt to drive better. To make sure I was OK, etc. Then they started to laugh about their times together. My children and I felt an uplift of spirit watching this.

But, as soon as they left an hour later, he literally collapsed on the bed. Shaman had to inject him with morphine.

"Why can't I see your father and Gurudeva yet? I need to see them. He is waiting for me." Shanky adored my Dad who had passed on to the other life in 2006. For him, my Dad was the kind of man he most wanted to be like.

I remembered that back in early September, Shanky had a dream where he met Sri Swami Satchidananda (Gurudeva). He was very excited about the dream. He said it was the first time he had dreamt of Gurudeva, and in the dream Gurudeva had told him that he was missing him and was so happy he was going home to him, and that he was waiting for Shanky. I was ecstatic when I heard that, as I had always wanted my husband to understand the relationship I had with my Guru. When he related the dream to me, I could feel the excitement and wonder in his voice. He actually seemed to have a direct connection with Gurudeva himself. I never for a moment thought that Shanky was foretelling his own death. I then had another flashback. In early August, Shanti and I had been to Barcelona to set up our charity with Marina. We were planning to build a school in Nepal. On the flight back home, I had a vision of me emptying out Shanky's wardrobes and giving all his clothes away. I remember I had to shake that vision off my mind and move on to something else. But it was always there, stored in the corner of my mind only to resurface at that moment. *Soon he will be gone, Nalanie. Three days. Make the most of each second.*

I started playing a CD of the mantra all the time, gently in the background. It made him smile. How odd life is. He used to get irritated with me for having mantras on all the time. He would say 'can't we listen to something else for a change?' Amidst the pain, I now smiled at the thought of him requesting mantras! When we were alone, I read the *Bhagavad Gita* to him, and some excerpts from *To Know Yourself* by Gurudeva. I would stroke his cheeks ever so lightly as he was in so much pain. I thanked him for all the years we had together. I thanked him for always taking care of my worst jobs, like expenses, accounting, bills etc. I told him how grateful I felt for our children and grandchildren. I thanked him for a life of adventure and meaning. I asked the children to go in one by one and talk to him, to say whatever they needed to say whilst he was still hearing us.

I was concerned how my grandchildren, the older two, Tara and Natasha would handle the situation. They spent a lot of time with Shanky and I. We were all early risers. Shanky would play puzzles and games with them so I could have my meditation time, which would usually last an hour. When I finished, I would chant a loud 'Om' and they would both come running into the little prayer room and meditate with me for a couple of minutes before they nudged me to give them breakfast. Oh, how grateful I was for the grandchildren! They brought so much light to my life and still do! They seemed to understand their Granddad was very sick and would gently creep into the room to see him quickly. We explained everything to them, as we did not believe in hiding the truth from the children. Children know things instinctively and hiding realities from them only creates fear in their little minds. They understood. They were quiet. They were trying to assimilate it all gently. They did not seem afraid.

I told Shanky that the family and Pico would be arriving on the 24th December. Shaman would take the car and pick them all up. Shanky just smiled and then fell asleep.

Monday morning, we could not wheel him into the sitting room. He was too tired. We spent the whole day with him in the bedroom, the whole family. Tuesday morning, I got out of bed with a heavy heart. I washed his face and body gently. He was not eating or drinking. We frequently dabbed his mouth with a soft cloth dipped in water. He hardly opened his eyes. My son's friends visited that afternoon and on seeing them I just burst out crying. I was very fond of my children's friends. They often had sleepovers in our place and we both loved it. Memories just flooded back to those wonderful years. Poor things, I don't think they knew how to react! But they were understanding and said, "Don't worry, Nalanie, all will be OK."

Tuesday afternoon, a friend we had not seen for ages, Anita, turned up with a huge pot of soup. I was so grateful, as none of us had any energy to even think about food except for the little ones.

8:20pm: My daughter and I sat together in the room drinking soup. Both of us with tears rolling down our cheeks. We held hands. We looked at Shanky. We looked at each other. We sat and prayed silently.

8:45pm: Shaman walked into the room. Father Paul from Gibraltar was calling to find out about Shanky. We placed the phone next to Shanky's ear and asked Father Paul if he could say a prayer. Shanky's eyes flickered and a hint of a smile appeared on his face. We felt grateful. Timing was perfect. Shaman left the room to check on the children.

9:00pm: Shani and I know. We don't know how we know. We looked into each other's eyes. Suddenly Shanky lifted his right hand as if to wave. At that moment Shaman walked into the room and all three of us heard Shanky take one deep breath and he was gone. Just like that. Like a puff of smoke. So peacefully. We all went close to him and started singing mantras. We all told him to go towards the Light and not to worry about us. We called the rest of the family in. I asked my grandchildren to stroke his hand and told them that Grandad had gone somewhere beautiful and there was no need to be afraid. We called Lulu. Andrew, my son-in-law, called the funeral home. He organized the coffin and they asked me what kind of coffin and what kind of flowers. I said the best of the cheapest coffins, as it was going to be turned into ashes anyway. Nevertheless, I wanted the most beautiful, colourful flowers to surround him. Then we just sang to him. It was surreal. It was a beautiful goodbye. We all thanked him for his love. I was so grateful that everyone was so calm at this crucial moment. It is said that excessive sobbing stops the soul's progress to the higher realms. We had discussed this earlier and all of us wanted Shanky to have the most amazing journey forward. He had suffered enough. His body was too sick and we had to let him fly. We would not be selfish. What can I say? It was the hardest moment of my life and yet the most beautiful of deaths. Was I crazy? Were we all crazy? The calmness and holiness that surrounded the bed is impossible to describe in words.

Lulu arrived and she showed the greatest of compassion, and I could see she was holding back her tears. She had grown to really love my husband and our family. She wrote out the death certificate and looked at us and said, "I have never seen a family like yours. You have all got together to show him so much love in his last moments and have let him go with such grace. This is the way it should be done."

Her words meant a lot to us.

I asked the boys, Andrew and Shaman, to stay in the room to help me bathe and dress Shanky. It was a sacred vigil for us. Shanky's body looked pristine and so young! How was this possible now that he has gone?

Truly unreal. We called the girls in to put his jacket on for him. They told us a few friends had arrived from Gibraltar and Spain. I was surprised. How did they get to know so quickly? I remember thinking at that time how kind they were to come all the way and give us moral support. Anita also returned and Shani asked her if she could serve tea and drinks to our guests. We asked Haresh, our Gibraltar lawyer and close friend, to put Shanky's tie on him. My mind was so fuzzy. The friends came in to see him. I took a shower and tried to get my head around things. I had to be strong to make decisions, and to be there for my family. The coffin arrived. They placed Shanky's body into it. And robotically I answered questions put to me.

"Yes, an open coffin. No, we will not cremate until after Christmas. I never want my family to associate Christmas with pain. Shanky would not want that. Christmas was his favourite time with the family. Make it the 26th December. Family on the flight from Hong Kong. Arriving tomorrow. I believe that the soul needs three days to integrate the loss of the body. I will stay in the morgue with the body. Shani will stay with me the first night. We cannot leave his body alone. Shaman will take us there and come back to sort out the technical paperwork." I started to sob. Friends in the sitting room. "Thank you for coming. Sorry I have to leave to be with my husband."

We left the apartment and for the next three days we slept at the morgue. My children and family helped me by taking it in turns to stay with the body so I could go home to shower. It was really quite beautifully arranged. The coffin was in a glassed iced room and we could see Shanky's body covered with the most amazing flowers of all colours. I felt sorry that the family members from Hong Kong had not arrived in time to say goodbye. But at least they could see him through the glass.

Oh, how my heart lifted when I saw my sister Mira and sister-in-law Avisha. They held me and comforted my broken soul. Shanky's sisters were sobbing unbelievably. They were in shock. They both had been told by their so-called 'Gurus' that Shanky would make it through the illness. In fact, before his death, when they phoned, they continuously related this to me. I was very irritated by it, as reality showed me otherwise. I urged them to come earlier, but they did not hear me. I have learnt that all those so-called predictions and promises were just 'pie in the sky'. I understood that they thought they were helping me. But honestly, it just made me more unstable. I felt sad for them but I was in too much pain myself to help them. All I could say to them was, "Please don't sob hysterically, as this will deter the soul's progress." I felt harsh for saying this because I knew they were suffering. "Cry softly."

So many times during those days I actually thought that Shanky would get up and walk. His face did not turn grey till just before the cremation. His skin looked alive and he did not need any make up at all. He looked so serene and at peace. How can I not be happy for him? I do not believe in death. I believe that the soul never dies. I know we are energy occupying the body. He was continuing his journey without me, as he was needed in other realms. How could I hold on to what was never mine in the first place? I was blessed he was my husband for 34 years. Gratitude mingled with agonizing pain in my heart. It was odd watching the 'ego' and the 'Self' but it was what kept me sane.

In the months and years that followed I realized how much understanding the conflicting emotions in me could serve, and have served others in the same predicament. Many came to see me when they lost someone in their lives. I could understand them. I had empathy. Questions like:

'Nalanie, was I responsible for his (or her) death? When I watched their terrible suffering, I asked God to relieve the agony. Was I too weak?'

'No,' I could answer. 'You were willing to let him (or her) go even though it meant that your life would be hell without them. You loved them tremendously and that is why you prayed for their release from suffering. It was a selfless prayer. Anyway, what makes you think that you have control over their time of death? You made the journey easier for them. Drop the guilt and focus on how blessed you were to be able to care for them and have them in your life.'

I watched the relief on the faces of those whose loved ones have been wrenched from their lives. I watched them pick up the broken pieces of their lives again. When counselling I have also used techniques in deep relaxation to enable them to forgive and to let go, and in conjunction with other mental, physical and spiritual exercises for them to work with. In time, with patience, they learn to live wholly again.

My husband's death was not futile. He chose to teach me so I could serve others. His sacrifice was awesome! When people thank me, I often tell them it is him they have to be grateful to.

'Accepting pain for purification, study of sacred scriptures and surrender to the Supreme Being (Consciousness) constitute yoga in practice.'

(Yoga Sutras of Patanjali, Book 2, Sutra 1)

Extract from the translation of this Sutra by Swami Satchidananda:

'The more you fire gold, the purer it becomes. Each time it goes into the fire, the impurities are removed. But, how can this burning process be effected with our mental impurities? By accepting all the pain that comes to us even though our nature is to run after pleasure. We will actually be happy to receive pain if we know its purifying effects. Such acceptance makes the mind steady and strong because, although it is easy to give pain to others, it is hard to accept without returning it. Such self-discipline cannot be practised in our meditation rooms, but only in our daily lives as we relate to others'

I was burning and willing to accept it.

Chapter 6
Time To Say Goodbye

Christmas morning arrived. Shanky's sisters and Pico very kindly volunteered to stay with the body whilst I went home to spend Christmas morning with the family. My family asked if I could deal with it emotionally to which I replied that Christmas was too important a day for Shanky and all our family for me to spoil. We sat down under the tree and distributed presents. None of us were in the mood but seeing the grandchildren excited to receive their gifts gave us the impetus we needed to get through it.

My mind was a blur. Nothing seemed to matter accept to maintain my strength for the family. I was Mom. If I fell apart, what good would that do for those living? I felt I would do my grieving later. I just wanted to get through Christmas and the funeral, and then I could let my guard down. There were so many phone calls. So many messages of condolence. People were so loving and sympathetic, but it was hard to speak. I did the best I could.

We got through it. We actually managed to all have a glass of wine that evening and drink to Shanky. The following day, 26th December, was the funeral at the crematorium where his body was kept. We had decided that we would have a memorial in Gibraltar on the 29th December at the Yoga Centre. The ceremony would be called 'a celebration of his life'. We thought that those who could not come to Spain could pay their respects at the Yoga Centre. In between those dates we would disperse his ashes. Shanky kept repeating how much he wanted to swim in the sea whilst he was ill so we felt that that was where his ashes should go. Shaman, Hersha, Shani, and Andrew organized both events for me. I asked them to say a few words. Shaman, Andrew and a few of Shanky's friends would speak for two minutes each. We chose the music. We wanted to make it beautiful for him. Shanky did not believe in rituals but he loved music. We chose his 'signature' song, which he always played on his guitar, 'Dream, dream, dream.'

All of us went to the funeral parlour early to say our final goodbyes to Shanky's body. The curators moved the coffin to the main chapel and placed it in the middle of the room. I felt numb. I said my goodbyes alone and then invited the rest of the family in. Was this really happening to us? I truly felt I was acting in a movie.

People started arriving. I had not expected so many! The chapel was overflowing. The whole service was special from beginning to end. Shaman spoke eloquently of his father, his friends talked highly of Shanky and then Andrew broke down as he was speaking and my daughter ran up and spoke for him. I was proud of her. I had not realized how close Andrew was to my husband. I got up as the service was ending and kissed Shanky's forehead. I offered flowers to those who walked up to the body to place on it before they closed the coffin. It was one of the most touching moments of my life. Watching people's faces and how much they loved my husband. I was thankful for this love. People hugged me and told me how sorry they were. I smiled through the tears that filled my eyes. "Thank you for coming. Thank you for being here for my Shanky. He would have loved this."

And then they took the coffin and put it into the incinerator. My heart sank. I would never see that body again. I just wanted to go home and sleep. I was exhausted but I could not rest yet. We had guests still with us and to attend the service in Gibraltar, which again, was beautiful, and even though it poured down with rain, the Centre was overflowing with people. The Gibraltar *sangha* members had organized the setting up of the hall for us. Everything was arranged exquisitely, flowers, candles and bookmarks to hand out. The children had made a beautiful video of his life and the final scene was of my son pouring the ashes onto the choppy sea and, at that very moment, a seagull swooped towards the ashes and flew up back into the sky. We all knew it was Shanky saying goodbye and he was letting us know he was flying. It was touching. The room was filled with love. The atmosphere was electric as the song *'Wind Beneath My Wings'* by Bette Midler played in the background. The service was a beautiful send off for my husband.

The story of the scattering of Shanky's ashes is worthy of telling as the seagull wasn't the only sign we received to comfort us that he was fine.

The day after the cremation, Shaman, Andrew and Pico all went to pick up the ashes and look for a boat that would take us out to the middle of the sea so that we could scatter them. The weather was horrific! Howling winds and rain. I felt the weather was mirroring my internal emotions. Shani, Hersha and I stayed to look after the grandchildren. Indira was tiny as she was only six months old, and although Talia, our special needs baby, was one and a half years old she looked even smaller. She was floppy and could not sit on her own, as her muscle tone was weak. She could not be left alone. My heart went out to Shani and Hersha. What wonderful mothers! They never complained and were there, just giving love. I sighed with gratitude.

I looked at Tara and Natasha who kept hugging me and saying "Granny, please don't be sad. Grandad loves you. We love you." These words meant so much to me coming from the little ones. My journey through loss and pain was made much easier because of them.

The boys came back without the ashes, as the curator told them it would take an hour or so more to place them in the urn. Yet, they looked really excited about something.

"Guess what Mom? We had a great sign today."

"Sign? What sign?" I asked.

"Remember Dad kept on saying he wanted to see your Dad?"

My father had passed away two years prior to Shanky. In such a short space of time I had lost the three most influential men in my life: First my Guru, then my father and now Shanky. It comforted me to know there was one thing my husband was looking forward to in dying, that he would see my Dad and Swami Satchidananda again.

"Well, we looked everywhere for a boat and nobody was willing to take us out today because of the weather. Then we saw this boat called 'Good Hope'. We walked up to it and seeing the owner there we asked him if he was able to take us out to scatter Dad's ashes. He agreed! Then we noticed the initials of the boat were GH, the same as your Dad, George Harilela! We got a sign! Your Dad is there to pick him up. What are the chances of something like that happening? And on top of it, look at the message, *Good Hope!*

I smiled. It lifted my spirit to know Shanky got his wish. The universe grants answers in many mysterious ways.

"We'll go collect the ashes now but still have a couple of hours till we get on the boat. What should we do with the ashes? Bring them home first?"

"Yes, absolutely," I replied. "We will all say a prayer over them before Dad goes on his way."

After the boys left my sister and sisters-in-law were very upset.

"Nal, you cannot bring those ashes to your home. According to the Hindu culture it is very bad luck for the family. I called the Hindu priest in Hong Kong and he reiterated that by no means should you allow them in your home."

I was shocked. "What? Are you kidding me? Shanky's ashes bad luck for us? What kind of nonsense and superstition is this? How can anyone tell me that my husband's ashes are bad luck! He only loved us all so much and there is no way that I will adhere to such nonsensical tradition. None of you have to be here when the urn arrives. You can be in your apartment. I understand that is what you believe, but me, no way will I succumb to this belief system. For me God is Love. And Shanky was Love to all of us."

They could see I was truly upset and decided to say no more. When the ashes arrived, I took the urn straight to my little prayer room and chanted some mantras and prayed for his soul to bathe in the Light and be free. My children and grandchildren said their prayers one by one. And to my surprise my sister Mira walked up to me and said, "You are very brave, Nal, to follow your own heart. You are right. God is Love. I would like to also say a prayer for Shanky."

My sister was very traditional so I was deeply touched by her magnanimous gesture. Then Avisha prayed. Then Pico. Then Shanky's sisters, Bhagwanti and Lavina. Each prayer was heartfelt and sincere. I wore an inner smile.

Over the years I had learnt this important lesson. When one feels strongly about something, even though everyone else disagrees with it, if one is brave enough to stick by their belief system, so long as it doesn't intentionally cause harm to anyone, in time, those that initially oppose you, will slowly understand your reasoning. And because of it, they make shifts in their own levels of conscious acceptance. The secret is to never expect anyone to agree with you and to accept that their views may not be yours. One should always respect that it is theirs and, to them, their truth.

This brings to mind a poster I had in my room as a teenager, which said:

I am not in this world to live up to your expectations.
You are not in this world to live up to mine.
You are you and I am I.
And if by chance we do meet,
It's beautiful.

Shanky's sisters and Pico left on the 30th December. Mira and Avisha left on the 2nd January. They wanted to stay to help me out but I told them that it was important they go home to their husbands and families. I told them not to waste any time on arguments and nonsense but to devote every moment they remembered with love. Life was too short. I pleaded not only with them, but also with all the couples I knew. Shanky and all the family had closure, as everything was enveloped with forgiveness, gratitude and love. That of itself gave us peace in the pain. We truly appreciated all the love and support we received.

The children received many signs during those days and for some time afterwards. One day they saw a mist in our bedroom. They were exhilarated. According to Buddhist scriptures, it is a sign that the soul has returned to let the family know it is fine. This was very reassuring for me. In the beginning I did not see the signs, as I was in too much pain. Pain blocks connection to the Source.

However, there was one huge sign that Shanky left me: his song. The one he wrote years before and sang at his 60th birthday party, the year of his death. The lyrics are as follows:

There is a world apart from the one, which we once knew.
And from this other side I can hear things clear and true.
And if I could reach out, I would touch you once again,
And make you realize there's no need to feel the pain.

I wish I could explain that I am with you every day,
And there's no reason why you should cry your life away.
Perhaps one day you'll see that I am still right here with you.
You'll wake up and suddenly you'll start your life anew.

Chorus:
Give me a sign if you hear me. One little sign will assure me.
Reach for me and you'll feel. Call to me and you'll hear.
I may have gone but I'm still right here beside you.
And wherever you go, let your happiness show
And remember, I love you.

The night that I left you, you broke right down and cried
But I never really went away I just came to the other side.
Perhaps one day you'll see that I am still right here with you.
You'll wake up and suddenly start your life anew.

(Chorus)

There'll be sunshine in the sky and you'll feel the morning dew.
And the birds that are singing everywhere are singing just for you.
Till then I'll stay with you. I'll always be right here.
You only have to call my name and your tears will disappear.

I wish you happiness and hope one day you'll find.
Another one to take my place and bring you peace of mind.
Till then I'll stay with you. I'll always be right here.
You only have to call my name and your tears will disappear.

Chorus:
Reach for me and you'll feel. Call to me and you'll hear.
I may have gone but I'm still right here beside you.
And wherever you go, let your happiness show.
And Remember.... I LOVE YOU.

(Lyrics and tune by Shanky Chellaram)

Six months later we recorded it in a professional studio with the singer Dennis Valerga, one of The Valerga Brothers who sang at Shanky's birthday party. The chorus was sung by my daughter, Shani and by my granddaughters, Tara and Natasha. We released it onto the Internet, as I wanted to share it with the world and especially with anyone who had suffered the loss of a loved one. They may have moved on from us physically but they remain forever in our hearts.

Loss, Life, Love

Book Two

Life

Chapter 1
Making Sense of Life

"Shaman, please can I sleep some more? I don't want to wake up. I am just so tired and would like to sleep for ten days." My body felt as if it was under a ton of bricks.

"Mom, I am sorry. But you really need to get up. We have to find you a new place to live. You can't stay here alone. It's too isolated. We need to move you closer to Shani and Andrew. We have an appointment to see the lawyer and go through all the paperwork. Don't worry, Mom. Dad and I organized as much as we could to make things easier for you after his passing. There is much to do, as Hersha, Indira and I were planning to leave by the end of the month. Do you want me to stay longer? Mom, I only want to make sure you are fine before we head back to Hong Kong."

"You are right, Shaman. No, you have already given up so much of your time to be here for Dad and I. You just moved to Hong Kong. You need to set up your business there and look after your family. I will shower and get ready right away. We can look at apartments today. I am just so appreciative that Hersha and you are here to help me out."

It was the 6th January. Mira and Avisha had left on the 2nd to see my brother Maj in Birmingham who was still suffering with throat cancer. I wish I could have gone with them. I was so worried about Maj. He called all the time whilst Shanky was in hospital, telling him to stay positive and that he could get over this. What about him now? Thank God he has Sara. I had no strength in my body to see him and my beloved sister Kantu in New Jersey. I received news that Vijay's health was deteriorating rapidly. She spoke with me after Shanky's passing but I felt it was too much for her. She was in shock. How could that be? Shanky was well when I was with her just two months before? I just silently prayed for them. Please bless my family.

We spent the next two days looking for the right apartment in Spain for me to move into. Shaman had already rented an apartment for me in

Gibraltar just in case I decided to go back there to live and to sort out all the legal issues that side of the border. But I was not ready to move back. I wanted to stay close to family, to Shani, Andrew and the girls.

We couldn't find anything that was reasonably priced and to my liking. I was very fussy about where I was going to live alone. Then Shaman suggested I move into a little apartment that Shanky and I had invested in just before the financial crash in 2008. We had paid a small deposit for it and were hoping to sell it and make a profit. We had a few arguments over it because when the market was buoyant we had some good offers for it but Shanky refused to sell thinking that the price would go up even more. The prices crashed that year.

The apartment was small and had two bedrooms and two bathrooms. It was a part of a brand-new development on the beachfront. We went to see it again.

"Mom, moving here makes a lot of sense. Andrew and Shani's office is right around the corner and their home is only five minutes away. You are between Gibraltar and Marbella so you can carry on your work with both *sanghas*. The apartment is walking distance to the shops. And besides, you are already paying the mortgage for it. Why go anywhere else and pay more?"

"Well, I was hoping to sell it and make a profit."

"You won't get the right price now and will lose whatever you have invested," Shaman answered.

Both my children were in the real estate business. Shaman was working with Andrew and Shani but when the crash occurred, he recognized that the business could no longer sustain two families. He then decided to move to Hong Kong to establish his own real estate business there.

"Its so small, Shaman. I have all the stuff from Gibraltar still in storage. I was hoping to empty that out and stop paying for the storage."

"There is a small storeroom in the underground parking that comes with this apartment."

"But there is no electricity and water connected yet. No Internet, no phone, no washing machine, no dishwasher, nothing!"

"I will help you get it all sorted before we go."

I looked around and asked Shaman to give me 24 hours to decide.

That night I asked the Divine for guidance and went to sleep. Whenever I had to make any big decision, I always prayed for help, that it would be the best for everyone and for myself. I prayed that things would be made clear to me. It was not about what I wanted or did not want. It was about what the Universe thought was best for me. That way I allowed my intuition to guide me rather than my analytical mind. It always worked. I woke up the next morning and instinctively knew that I should move to *La Noria*, the name of the Urbanization where the small apartment was situated. That is why it did not sell. Shanky's psyche knew that it was where I should be. The location was perfect. I went straight to Shaman and told him we would start the process immediately. He asked if I was sure and I answered in the affirmative.

Everything just flowed in the weeks that followed. We could feel the Divine Consciousness guiding us all the way. Water and electricity were installed amazingly quickly, in a matter of days! In Spain it could sometimes take weeks. We shopped for furniture and appliances for the kitchen. Whatever I owned we moved to La Noria. Whatever I did not need I just gave away. I asked Andrew and a friend by the name of Ole to take whatever they liked of Shanky's clothes and the rest we gave to a charity shop. I also distributed Shanky's collection of books, DIY equipment and other items to whoever wanted them. I gave away a lot of cutlery and silverware that I had never used to those who were thrilled to have them.   There was a young couple just about to set up a new home but had no furniture or car. I gave them most of the furniture and whatever they needed for their new home. I sold my secondhand car to them cheaply so I could buy myself a new one. Yucks! I dreaded the thought of driving!   Meanwhile Shaman used Shanky's Honda to take us everywhere. Hersha was running around with baby Indira and I will never forget the vision of her sitting in the La Noria apartment on boxes and feeding her baby and she never complained. We went into the local household store and I just picked whatever we needed quickly. Light fittings, showerheads, curtains, appliances. All done in a couple of hours.

Shaman kept asking me, "Mom are you sure? You're choosing things quickly without too much thought!"

"I want to move in before you leave. I am choosing things that I really feel will look good in the new apartment. I don't want to spend a lot, as I don't know when I'll move again. We are so blessed that everything is on sale at the moment. And you know it is not in my nature to waste time by overthinking."

We hired Shaman's friend, Andy, to help us with all the electrical and plumbing connections. Shaman worked hard to install a shower unit in the second bathroom. Bit by bit everything started coming in. The deadline was to move me in by the 28th January. Shaman and Hersha would spend one night with me before leaving, to make sure I was alright. During this time, we also saw lawyers, sorted bank accounts, changed joint names on legal papers into my sole name, sorted furniture, packed boxes, and so on. It kept me busy and exhausted so I was able to fall asleep easily. It was a horrible time. The internal pain was excruciating but I had to carry on. I thought that once they left, I would sit down and give myself time to grieve. I knew that I needed to really allow myself to go over my life with Shanky in my mind, in order to absorb the pain and then release it. I understood fully that this was a process and I needed to be alone to go through it.

For me, the worst part was sorting out the financial issues. I realized how fortunate it was that Shanky did not have much in his name, as when he wanted to sell the family shop in Gibraltar his father and brother refused to sign the papers unless Shanky gave them 65% of his shares. I remember being so angry over this, but I encouraged my husband to accept these conditions because otherwise it could have gone on for years and the shop had been losing money daily. I quoted the old English saying at him, 'a bird in the hand is worth two in the bush.' I think back now and I can see the perfect Universal plan. If he hadn't sold his shares, I would have been involved in a nightmarish situation with his family. I had sold my dream home in Gibraltar, the one given to me by my father, so we would have enough to live on. This turned out to be the right decision. After it was sold and we moved to Spain Shanky told me he had the best two years of his life! Throughout my life I have seen this pattern. What I believed was a difficult situation at that time would always turn out for the best in the future. This repetitive experience gave me the confidence and trust that life always worked out for the best in the end.

The words of my Guru rang in my head:

It's all Its form.
It's all Its name.
It's all Its deed.
And it's all for Good.

My father had always said to me, *'God's plan is perfect.'* Now these precious words kept me sane and focused even though I felt like a walking zombie. As I said earlier, I was shocked by the pain I felt. I kept wondering how people got through this without spiritual knowledge!

On the 28th January, when everything was almost completed, our friends Haresh and Anju organized for us all to go out for dinner at a beachfront restaurant, which was walking distance from the apartment. Andrew chose the restaurant, as he had promised Shanky that when he sold his next property, he would treat him and the family to a delicious dinner there. From that day onward we decided that if we wanted to go anywhere and could afford it, we would never wait but instead do it immediately. It was the first time I had gone out for dinner after Shanky's death. It felt strange to dress up and put make up on. Dress for whom? But I did it and we all managed to stay positive and smile even though our hearts were breaking. We were thankful that Anju had insisted and refused to take no for an answer! It helped us get back to reality. Ha! What is reality?

Shaman, Hersha and Indira left the following day. In a way I was looking forward to having the space to grieve alone but at the same time it was so hard to see them go. Shaman had been my rock and strength. Would I be able to deal with the final documents and all the visits to the lawyers to sort out the probate? Would I be able to drive my new car home alone from Gibraltar? I hadn't driven that distance on my own for over 20 years! I knew if I wanted, I could call any of the Yogis and they would run to help me. Something in my soul kept saying, *'Nalanie, you have to learn to be independent otherwise you will always live in fear, and then you will not respect yourself. What kind of Yogi are you anyway? Don't you remember Gurudev's words?*

'Faith and fear do not go together'.

I told myself, *'Get a grip on yourself, girl'.*

Due to the continuing economic crisis, Shani and Andrew were going through tough times and had to downsize their business. At the same time they had to deal with Talia's health problems. In fact, they had to be in Barcelona that very week for her muscle biopsy, which we all dreaded.

That evening I was alone for the first time in the new apartment. It surprised me that it did not feel strange. In fact, it felt warm and cosy. I sat down on the brand-new sofa pondering on the meaning of life once more. What was my purpose for being now? What was the point of anything? Thirty-four years with a person makes you almost one with them. Who am I now that I am no longer a wife to Shanky? Where was the God I loved so much? Why did Shanky have to leave so young and just as he was finding himself in a world without having to work in a shop and worrying continuously? Should I continue living in Spain? Should I return to Hong Kong and be with my Mom who never truly recovered emotionally after my Dad's passing two years earlier? Or should I move to Barcelona? I loved that city and my friend Marina lived there. Should I take up monkhood and devote my life to meditation and prayer? Oh, Shanky, I miss you terribly but I don't want to hold you back from your forward journey! I know you are free but I am not yet. I stopped myself from thinking too much. *Om Shanti, Om Shanti, Om Shanti. Peace to all. Peace to the pain. Peace to Shanky. Peace to my family. Peace to my children and grandchildren. Peace to all the sangha members and all my wonderful friends. Peace.*

And I cried myself to sleep.

Chapter 2

Bereavement

Over the years I have coached many through their bereavement process. I have even cried with them and held their hands. I have watched them heal. Each in their own time and in their own way. Each one I counselled was different, but the tools I shared with them were the same. We would sit and discuss death and how we all had to leave the world one day. I asked them to read books on death and dying so they would understand their own process and not feel they were victimized. I taught them how to breathe deeply when in pain, to watch comedies to uplift themselves, to meditate and most of all to accept that they had been left behind because there was something they were still required to do or learn whilst remaining on this earth. My master had taught me that we need three things to live a beautiful life:

> To be peaceful
> To be easeful
> To be useful

In order to be peaceful, I taught them how find serenity in pain. Breathing, practising gratitude for what they had, and some creative visualizations, such as seeing themselves peaceful and smiling even though they did not feel it. To breathe deeply every time the pain felt too much. To speak with someone close to them about their feelings and not to be embarrassed by their tears. To never stop speaking about the person who had passed on. They may have left their bodies, but their energies would always be around in our minds and hearts. For some, acceptance of death often took a long time. However, this was *before* I experienced the loss of my husband. *After* the loss of my husband, I noticed something very interesting. Acceptance for many of my clients came much quicker. When they saw me smile and laugh and carry on even though I had a constant ache in my heart, it made them feel they could also do it! And it was therapeutic for me too. As I rallied them forward, the better they felt the lighter I became. It was the empathy with my loss that they were experiencing, and somehow it made them heal faster.

To be easeful, I taught them some Yoga postures and meditation techniques. I recommended they take a walk every day as it really does raise endorphin levels, which makes us feel happier. Whilst grieving and going through all the legal paraphernalia they had to deal with, I advised them to gently pace themselves and not take too much on in one day. I had found that dealing with matters such as probate, death duties, taxes, accounts, insurance companies and banks all too consuming of my energy and strength at a time when I needed them the most. I really could not understand why governments would put us through so much paperwork when we are grief-stricken and really need things to be simplified. Some of our laws seemed ludicrous! How could public administration be so cruel and unsympathetic?

To feel useful in life is vital. After being with one person for many years whether a husband, wife, partner, sibling, parent or friend, there is a strong connection. When that physical connection is broken it can lead one to a feeling of emptiness, which can often result in despondency. It almost feels as if one has lost a limb. Suddenly there seems no reason to live. No reason to be on earth. I have seen this attitude particularly in people who have been carers for a long time. Whilst looking after a sick or disabled person in their care, they frequently found themselves wishing they could have their freedom back, and often felt frustrated and stressed out. When that sick or disabled person then leaves the body, instead of feeling a sense of relief that the person they cared for is finally free from suffering, they are overcome by guilt and remorse. They punish themselves for having had those thoughts. So I explained to them that it was perfectly normal to think that way and they never meant anything harmful by their thoughts, and that when exhaustion takes over the mind goes to strange places! I sympathized and reiterated how unbearable it is to watch suffering. We are only human, and humans experience various thoughts and emotions. I taught them how to release their guilt by processing themselves through the use of self-forgiveness tools. Understanding that just because one thinks a thought it does not imply they are that thought. This could take up to three sessions of therapy, but most got it in one. However, I also advised them to continue to attend my public talks, or other talks given by people who could inspire and help them to understand death and dying. To discover for themselves their life's journey, and to educate themselves by reading books on spiritual topics.

What is spirituality anyway?

Biologically we are made up of atoms, and atoms are energy. Our physical bodies carry electrical currents. Simply notice the static we experience on a cold day when touching a metal item. Or the electricity in hair when you travel on long flights. Notice the heat that builds up in the body when meditating. When our energy levels are low, we feel lethargic. When high, we feel active. I often ask my students these questions: 'who, or what, were you before you came into this body? What leaves the body when it dies?' Some call it *soul*, others call it *prana, chi* or *qi*. These expressions simply mean the same thing, *life force.* Next I ask: 'who are you, then? Are you the body or the energy that resides in the body?' Some get it immediately and others look at me blankly. It really depends on their belief system. If they are religious, they know they are *soul*. If they are spiritual, they connect with the fact that they are *prana,* or energy. If they have no belief system, they start thinking about these truths and gradually, in time, accept the concept of *Consciousness*.

In the last ten years my work has been made much easier by the progress made in the fields of Neuroscience and Epigenetics. Following a great deal of scientific experimentation significant evidence has materialized to show how the brain works and how meditation practices can help rewire our thinking process. MRIs taken before meditation and after meditation have clearly shown how the areas of the brain that deal with emotions have become relaxed, and literally light up. The concept of changing thoughts this way is not new. It has always been taught in the Yogic scriptures, which date back more than 3,000 years! Yet the nature of Homo sapiens is to doubt unless empirically proven. The surge forward in science is finally connecting the dots to spirit, and both are joining at the same point.

I have learnt that to be spiritual is to know that we are all part of a whole. That all things are sacred, and when we live in harmony with mankind, nature and especially ourselves, we start to know we truly are 'a divine spark' and so is everything else. We just vibrate at different frequencies depending on the way we think and live. When we experience this *oneness* we feel bathed in peace. We realize that truly all life is a stage and we are but actors on it. Once we know that, we can determine how we want to live in the circumstances we are given. We can be bitter and angry if we choose, but what does that do for anyone, especially ourselves? Or, we can decide to accept the situation and make the most of it. Then, not only do we benefit ourselves, but also everyone else.   A win/win situation!   And where is God in all of this? The ancient Yogic scriptures, called *The Vedas*, put it this way:

'Ekam sat vipraa bahuda vadanti.'

This means, *'Truth is one, the wise call it by different names'.*

People often ask me, 'Is there a God?' And I answer that, for me, yes, absolutely there is! But my interpretation of God is possibly different from yours. For me God is the light in all of us and in all things animate and inanimate. It is illumination *Itself* and when we connect with *It*, we experience bliss. My favourite definition of 'It' is, *The Lord of Love, no larger than a thumb, lives in the hearts of all.* (From *The Upanishads.*)

If you look at our human body and the way it works, it is a phenomenal machine.   Just observe how the earth moves on its axis and is round, and how gravity keeps us from flying off as it spins.   And then consider, what about all of nature and how things work in it?   How is it we have day and night, and the seasons, the cyclical pattern to which all of nature moves?   How did the sun and moon get to where they are? Surely, there must have been some kind of designer if there is a design? Is it all down to evolution? What caused existence in the first place? So many questions! To date it seems there are thousands of theories but no real, definitive answers.   However, quantum physics, a relatively new science, now asserts that *Consciousness* is everywhere.   In doing so, science is ostensibly catching up with spirituality, with what has been known for millennia. The philosophy of Yoga has always stated there to be a Grand Design, that *Consciousness* is the creator and the force behind absolutely everything.

I have come to understand that we cannot know God with our minds but we can experience what we call 'God' through certain practices that awaken *kundalini* (the dormant spiritual force in our subtle body), which sometimes arouses spontaneously.   The great Masters, Lord Jesus, Lord Buddha, Shankacharya, Patanjali, Swami Satchidananda, and many more, have taught us about the 'Middle Path', the path to truth, the path of light. "Look within, the kingdom of heaven is within." Walking in their footsteps, we encounter our true selves, the one that abides in the body. The sages tell us that when we understand the microcosm, we will understand the macrocosm. When I heard my master say, "Make peace your God and don't even allow God to disturb your Peace" something in my consciousness shifted and I discovered a *new* God, a God that is one of pure unconditional love. Gone was the God who loved you when you were good and punished you when you were bad. Gone was that God that proclaimed we were born with original sin. I discovered instead the owner of the theatre who made me both a director and actor for this drama called *My Life*! The backdrop was my given set: where I was born, who my parents were, my genetic heritage, my personality, and so on. My destiny would be determined by how well - or otherwise - I played my role.

> *'You are what your deep, driving desire is.*
> *As your desire is, so is your will.*
> *As your will is, so is your deed.*
> *As your deed is, so is your destiny.'*

> (Brihadaranyaka 4, 4.5, The Upanishads
> Interpreted by Eknath Easwaran)

During this play I will see both heroes and villains, and at the end of the play, when the show is over, we will all sit together and enjoy a glass of wine! It became clear that our life's work was to live to the best we could be, to live a peaceful life so that we can benefit the world around us and not disturb it. We are not here only for ourselves. We are here to work with our earth brothers and sisters to create a better and happier world for all. Albert Einstein explained it succinctly:

"A human being is a part of a whole, called by us 'universe', a part limited in time and space. He experiences himself, his thoughts and feelings as something separated from the rest... a kind of optical delusion of his consciousness. This delusion is a kind of prison for us, restricting us to our personal desires and to affection for a few persons nearest to us. Our task must be to free ourselves from this prison by widening our circle of compassion to embrace all living creatures and the whole of nature in its beauty."

When you shift your thought pattern from '*why me?*' to '*why not me?*', from victimhood to empowerment, from selfishness to selflessness, healing can occur simultaneously.

I found myself using all the tools that I had shared with others all those years, on myself. I was extremely grateful to the people who came to me in their darkest moments for help. It is because of them that I could see perfectly clearly what the pitfalls were on this path of sorrow. I was able to watch myself as a subject.

I spent many evenings sitting down in front of the TV both crying and laughing at the same time. Crying because I was in pain and I allowed myself to grieve. Laughing because I was watching the US TV series called *Friends*, a wonderful and hilarious sitcom. I was so grateful to my son for the TV he installed for me. It really did see me through those dark, sad evenings. I thought I would feel alone, but I did not. I felt Shanky's presence strongly. I felt the love from all my family, friends and *sangha* members with me. This gave me a very strong foundation. I learnt that in order to heal fully, I had to allow myself to feel the pain intensely and I am happy to say it did not kill me but instead initiated me into deeper wisdom. The wisdom to recognize how short life really is. The wisdom of not wasting time on non-essentials. The wisdom of being truthful to how I felt and not worry about what others thought. I remember telling all the couples I knew or who came for my counsel not to waste time with silly quarrels. To spend more time in gratitude, in romance! All life should be a Divine Romance! Let people know you care and love them. This makes life feel rich and abundant. Our daily life is our laboratory where we can fine-tune our thought patterns and experiment on ourselves. What a gift this body is, as it houses the spirit, and how wonderful to play the Divine role for the sake of the Greater Consciousness!

The sixth week after Shanky's passing was the hardest. I knew it would be. I was thankful that I was prepped for it. I learnt this lesson when my children were young. Whenever they went back to boarding school after a long holiday, I would find that for the first five weeks I would miss them but be perfectly okay. By the sixth week, I was aching to see them. I later noticed this six-week sequence in couples that separated. They would celebrate for the first 5 weeks and then towards the sixth week they would become weepy, depressed and start wondering if they had done the right thing. Similarly, when detoxing it was recommended to keep it up for at least six weeks. And following an operation it was usually suggested to wait six weeks before intense exercise could be reintroduced.

And I noticed for bereavement cases, almost on the dot, the sixth week was when most broke down completely from the intensity of the pain.

Prior to that time, something in their psyche would secretly hope that all of it was a dream and the deceased person would literally rise from the dead and appear to them. But when that did not happen, the reality of never seeing that person physically ever again became a reality almost too hard to bear.

No matter how ready I thought I was, I still felt the onslaught of the pain. I had woken up during the night and reached out to hug Shanky and he was not there. My hands groped in the dark and all I felt were the cold sheets. I sat up and rocked myself back and forth telling myself that it was OK, that this horrific pain would pass. But the tears would not stop. I looked at the empty bedroom and shouted, "Shanky, I just need to know if you are alright. Where you are? Are you with the Light or is it all darkness? Please, please give me a sign."

As a child, I was psychic. I used to see things and hear voices, which would scare me terribly. Many a night I would wake my eldest sister Mira up, trembling with fright. She would tell me to jump in her bed and hug me till I fell asleep again. These visions went on for years until two months after I gave birth to Shani, when I saw a vision of my grandmother who had passed a few days earlier in Hong Kong. I was stuck in Gibraltar and could not attend her funeral, which made me feel woeful. She smiled so sweetly at me and said she loved me and could I buy her flowers. It was 3am. I was delighted to see her and then suddenly panic gripped my heart. I woke Shanky to tell him I had seen her but the initial feeling of happiness had inexplicably turned to one of terror. Why? I did not understand myself so at that moment I prayed that I would never see anything again, and if there was a message for me then please have it manifested in a dream instead. And that is exactly what happened in the years that followed. I received messages in dreams, messages that were truly significant. And I still do. I feel energies and vibrations strongly. I feel auras and energy fields. I hear music and sounds but I no longer see 'beings', what some may term as 'ghosts' but I prefer to call them 'visions'. I still see sparkles, lights seemingly without source, and almost imperceptible mists, and the fall of rain on cloudless sunny days. But with Shanky's passing, I wanted to see *him*. I wanted him to appear in bodily form. But no such thing happened.

I found out that so many felt the same way after a loss. Then I would say to them: "If I asked your partner to materialize right here, right now, will you promise me you would not be scared?" They would invariably admit they would be terrified at which point I would calmly say, "that's why they don't appear. They know that!"

I got up and made myself a cup of coffee wondering how I could remove this vicious pain that felt as though I was about to have a heart attack but, of course, I knew all along was simply heartbreak. I then decided to have a hot bath. A good soak in a hot tub always made me relax and feel better. Yes, I would put some nice smelling oils in the water and just lie back and enjoy it. Whilst in the bath, I kept thinking of Shanky and the life we had together when suddenly the whole bathroom became ablaze with a bright white-yellow light that pulsated. This went on for over twenty minutes and I knew it was Shanky, and he had come to tell me that he was in the light. I cannot even start to explain this vivid experience. There are no words for it. Waves of peace gushed through my body and my being was filled with both awe and gratitude. And from that moment I understood I would have to carry on without him the best I could. The words of his song rang through my head.

'Reach for me and you'll feel,
Call to me and you'll hear,
I may have gone but I'm still right here beside you.
Give me a sign if you hear me. One little sign will assure me.
And wherever you go, let your happiness show,
And remember, I love you.'

And I spoke out loud to that light. "I feel you and I hear you. I understand you are in light and must continue your journey. I promise to do the utmost with the rest of my life on earth. What is left for me to do now is truly, "serve, love, give, meditate, purify, realize, do good, be good and I will do it for you, with your name in my heart." This became my mantra in the months to follow. I knew that the road to healing would take time. I had to embrace the pain and that, in the end, all would be well. I just had to be patient. I accepted it all and now all I had to do was allow time to do its healing work.

Chapter 3
Death The Teacher

'Soul surgery without anaesthetic can be extremely painful'
(From *Divine Grace* - Chapter16)*

The first time I did anything on my own without Shanky was always the most painful. Driving my new car had me break down in sweat and tears. After that, I promised myself I would just have to be bold. I never wanted to put myself in such horrible dread again! Going to places we had been together was especially hard. I vowed that by the end of the first year following his passing I would visit all these places to get it out of my system.

Going to the bank to close his account resulted in a barrage of tears. The poor bank assistant, she really had no idea what to do or say! I called myself 'Mrs Waterworks' in order to lighten the situation, at least in my mind. I remember so clearly going to the supermarket to buy a pack of six large bottles of water. After I paid at the checkout desk, I went to lift the bottles and I found that I couldn't. They were too heavy! Tara my granddaughter, who happened to be with me, saw me cry and quickly took over and said, "Gran, I can carry them."

I looked at her little form and said, "Tara, it's OK. I just have to become stronger and once I stop crying it will be easier."

She just grabbed the bottles from the counter and lifted them easily into the shopping trolley. "See Gran, I may be small but I am stronger than you. Gran, don't worry. I will always help you with the water and heavy stuff. You never have to cry for that."

Those words, coming from her, were so endearing. I gave her a big hug.

*Divine Grace was a book of affirmations and poems I had published in 2012

It's funny how this simple scene has always played in my head, and made me feel protected and swell up with love. After that I decided to have a filtered water tap installed in the apartment so I would not have to buy heavy packs of water ever again. Best thing I did. From every adversity comes some good!

Particularly hard was going to the cinema again. Every Thursday afternoon Shanky and I would go to the cinema and watch whatever movie was playing that took our fancy, eat popcorn and then go out for a meal. It was one of our favourite pastimes. It was the last thing on the list that I had to face up to and overcome. I kept putting it off. One year later, on New Year's Day, a group of Yogis joined me and supported me in the endeavour to remove the dread I had felt and to rekindle my love for the cinema. I was totally honest and told them how I felt. I must admit, because more than a year had elapsed, it was actually easier than I thought it would be. There were no tears. I remember thinking, 'Darling, I am enjoying this for you. I am truly recovering.' I could feel him smile at me.

The reason I mention this episode is that, whilst counselling others for bereavement, I had learnt it was the same for the majority of people. They dreaded returning to places they had visited with their late loved ones. Many were not as fortunate as I had been, to move out of the apartment Shanky and I rented. They stayed in their homes where everything reminded them of the person they had lost. Many were so attached to their partner's personal effects such as clothes, shoes, personal toiletries, etc. Giving them away to friends or donating them to charity was really a very hard task for some. The longer they took, the more they suffered. I told them to hang on to a few items for comfort but not more. I had to guide them through this distressing process. When they finally achieved it, they actually shocked themselves by the relief they felt.

Other techniques to help them to heal included encouraging them to visualize a time when they would feel laughter again from deep within, and reminding them they had other family members to live for. I would plot a timeline to prepare them so that the shock from the severe emotions they would experience could be lessened. As the saying goes, 'prevention is better than cure'.

The timeline would generally look like this:

1.) *First five weeks:* The feeling of living under a dark cloud where nothing makes sense. Everything feels surreal. One feels like a zombie, running on automatic, doing things because they have to and not because they want to. Anger in some. Feeling victimized and punished. Memory loss. All this can go on for some time, even way past the first year if help is not sought.

2.) *The 6th to 12th week:* The pain becomes quite unbearable. Panic, anxiety, fear keep coming up. Deep depression can set in if one does not seek immediate counselling or help. What can be a dangerous period. Everything seems bleak. Constant heartache. No desire to wake up and face the day.

3.) *After the third month:* Periods of relief from pain start to transpire. If the relationship was a troubled one then regrets, guilt and blame ensue. If a good relationship, the feeling of deep gratitude mixed with deep sadness. A terrible feeling of loneliness is born.

4.) *From the 4th to 6th month:* There will be a slight easing but the fear of never being truly happy again fills the heart unless one is inspired by the work they are doing, or by family members and close friends.

5.) *The remainder of the first year:* All important days, such as birthdays, anniversaries and holidays, will be especially tough. The feeling of being nauseous when these days come up is very normal. This can carry on throughout one's life but as the years pass the intensity of emotion becomes lessened. It's important to be around someone close on these days.

The above timeline is just a guide. There are no hard and fast rules. Each emotion can shift one onto another and may last longer depending on the individual. However, all the clients I have seen, and still see, have found the timeline helpful. For example, when a birthday was approaching and the distress levels increased, they would call me to get assurance that this was a normal process and they would get through it. Without doubt, every single case that I worked with did manage to get through it. The use of breathing techniques with the affirmation 'this too shall pass' seemed to relax them through this disturbing phase.

I learnt by watching my own emotions. It was thanks to the Yogic practices I had followed for over twenty years that gave me the strength that was needed. I refused to let sorrow overcome me but instead embraced my feelings by allowing them to be expressed when the sorrow surfaced. There was an awareness that I was never alone and that a mystical force was constantly with me, holding me. Throughout my soul's journey on this earth, I have held a firm conviction that I had no right to disturb anyone's peace. So, on the days that I felt unwell, I would stay quietly at home till the gloomy mood left me. I had meditated every day without a break and I continued my practice after Shanky passed. I noticed that whilst in sorrow, the meditation was stark, it did not uplift me as I thought it would. However, I never stopped these practices. I had learnt from my Master that one would just have to drive themselves through these dark nights of the soul. I held no doubts that it would pass. Patience was the key. My work now was to support those lost in their darkness to redeem their light. And, the way I could do that was to share what I had ascertained.

'Spiritual awakening is knowing we are more than the body and to prepare oneself for the eventuality of death.'
(From *Divine Grace* – Chapter 16)

I always recommend reading books on death and dying to those about to lose a loved one, and the reason I do so, morbid though it may sound, is that it is important to understand the process the dying person is going through. It is imperative that we comfort them through this transition from being in this world to leaving it. It can be frightening for many. Understanding the process not only helps the person who is dying but also those witnessing their passing at that time. It also assists the witnesses with the healing process afterwards. I found it helped me greatly, as Shanky and I were able to have closure. There were no lingering regrets.

In order to help a dying person we need for a while to put ourselves 'in their shoes'. Although there are many ways to leave this earth, I shall use the example of someone dying from either a terminal illness or simply from old age. Imagine that you are about to leave everything you have ever known. Your body, which has been with you throughout your life, your family, friends, home and all your possessions. Then one by one you lose all your abilities. Muscular control is no longer in your hands and the next thing you know is that you are incontinent and you need to wear nappies (diapers) or insert a catheter. You feel you have lost your dignity and that it is demeaning. Next, everyone tells you what you need to do or eat even though you may dislike it all intensely. It is their version of love but it's often difficult to see it that way. You not only lose your independence, you also start feeling guilty that people around you have suspended their normal day-to-day activities to look after you. You are no longer able to walk, your hearing becomes worse, it becomes harder to speak, you are sleeping more and are afraid to say what you really feel so that you don't hurt your family. At the same time, you have hallucinations as you slip in and out of consciousness, and you are unsure if there is anything beyond when you take your last breath.

This is what happened to my husband and I made sure that my children and I gave him the soul medicine that he needed. I spoke to him of the light. I read to him passages that talked about the afterlife and reincarnation. We spoke about love and the beautiful children and grandchildren he was leaving behind in the world. We spoke about all the wonderful things he achieved and the mistakes that were made. I explained we all made many mistakes and it was just part of our human journey. The amazing thing is that he heard and he did forgive so much in those final days. He developed spiritual wisdom beyond anything I could have imagined during my life with him. The aura around him was peaceful. Visitors could not believe he was so sick as he glowed. He believed without doubt that he would meet my Dad and my Spiritual Master. We surrounded him with love and mantra music and he would hum along with it. I instructed him to focus his attention on the higher centres of his astral body, namely the heart, throat, forehead and crown of the head, when he felt he was about to leave the body. According to Yogic scriptures these are the better exit points for the soul, as it takes them to the higher realms. I advised him to keep his attention towards the clear, white light and not focus on leaving us behind. His death was truly one of the most peaceful I had ever seen. This gave us all the closure we needed to continue with our lives. By studying the process of dying from the many traditions and religions, I was provided with the knowledge I needed to see us through this most difficult time. Now I advise all my students to study and read about death and dying so we can all prepare not only others but also ourselves for this most crucial moment.

All traditions and religions have one thing in common. That during the last moments one should focus on God, whatever their version of God may be, and that is why a holy person is called upon to visit the one who is dying. Whatever your faith may be, or even if you have no faith, it is comforting to know someone is with you, guiding and helping you through the final transition.

Death taught me many phenomenal lessons. That whilst we are going through negative emotions the connection to God or the Divine Consciousness is obscure. We can even become disconnected. I learnt that when I was in peace, tranquillity and acceptance I could get reconnected. I had always known this. But now I knew that I knew. The only way I could recover this peace was to continuously remind myself that Shanky was not dead. He had just gone to 'the other side'. I hung on to the vision of light I had seen in my bathroom. When my heart was filled with love the connection with being alive and fulfilled became illuminated. When waves of love emanated through my body the bliss I thought I had lost returned. It was my grandchildren that reignited this love in me! Their innocent faces with their beautiful smiles lit up my life. They were my medicine and I was indebted to my daughter and my son for sharing them so lovingly with me.

Death also taught me that God was unconditional love, and vice versa. I came to understand and accept that Shanky had to give up his life so that I could learn this truth and help others on their road through suffering. Death taught me that, as painful as it was, his passing was so that I could grow. And death taught me that Shanky was truly my Guru and the reason why I am writing this book.

She Is Gone: *A poem by David Harkins*

You can shed tears that she has gone or smile because she lived.
You can close your eyes and pray that she will come back or you can open your eyes to see all she has left.
Your heart can be empty because you can't see her or you can be full of the love you shared.
You can turn your back on tomorrow and live yesterday or you can be happy for tomorrow because of yesterday.
You can remember her only that she is gone or you can cherish her memory and let it live on.
You can cry and close your mind, be empty and turn your back or you can do what she'd want: smile, open your eyes, love and go on.

Chapter 4
Service The Healer

'The dedicated ever enjoy supreme peace, so live only to serve'
(Swami Satchidananda)

I realized I had to carry on with the job of living. It was time to get back to work. I knew returning to Gibraltar would be difficult. My weekly itinerary included giving *satsang* (talk on spirituality) every Tuesday in Spain and on Wednesdays in Gibraltar. Two countries separated by a land border. I would spend the whole day at the Integral Yoga Centre in Gibraltar, seeing patients and then giving a discourse on the philosophy of Yoga at 6pm. I knew I would be stopped on my way to the centre by people offering their condolences. Both Shanky and I were well known. I decided to 'bite the bullet.' It was hard but I did it. People really meant well and they truly cared. It was I who was still sensitive. Without failure, true to *Its* energy, the Divine sent me assistance. As I was walking towards the Centre Sheila, the wife of my doctor Peter Borge, saw me and automatically came towards me, put her arm through my arm and said to hold on to her. She was a pillar of strength for me that morning. She didn't say much. That was wisdom on her part. As Mother Teresa would say, 'We cannot do great things, but we can do small things with great love.' These small acts of kindness without expectation are what a person who is in mourning needs. Conversation can prove challenging.

I called Paddy and Shanti who both acted voluntarily as my personal assistants. Paddy handled my counselling appointments in Gibraltar and Shanti was assisting with my international work. They were overjoyed to hear I was getting back to work by the end of February. Lakshmi, who was vice-chairperson of the Centre, held the fort in Gibraltar during my absence. She was relieved at my return, as all the responsibility of running the Centre had been on her shoulders. I was blessed to be working alongside such great souls. They and many of the *sangha* members played a huge part in my healing process. As soon as I walked through the door of the Integral Yoga Centre, the heaviness evaporated. Seeing the faces of Julio, our treasurer and good friend, Paddy, Shanti, Lakshmi. Les, Karen, Jasmine, Anju, Bhavani, Rasmi, Geeta, Daya and all the other yogis waiting there to hug me and show me their support was overwhelming. Their love gave me great fortitude. There were a few people waiting to see me for private consultations. At 6pm, I was due to enter the main hall to give a public talk. The room was full to capacity. The audience stood up and held the *Namaste* gesture as I passed them to get to the altar. Their glances spoke of their compassion and love. The title of the talk for the evening was 'Parting is such sweet sorrow'. The words just flowed out as I candidly related my journey through grief and how I looked at life and death. I expounded how nobody ever died and death was just a door to a new life. It was this truth that sustained me. There was not a dry eye in that hall. They felt my pain and rejoiced at the God given strength I exhibited, and I rejoiced along with them. After I had finished speaking, those in the audience who had lost a loved one approached me and expressed their gratitude. They felt I had given them some gems of wisdom that would help them move forward from their own grief.

By the end of that day I realized that I was still useful and that inspired me considerably. After leaving the Centre I crossed the border and met Shani and Andrew for dinner, and was relieved that I had made it into Gibraltar and back to Spain driving on my own. I realized that evening that I suffered from astigmatism and that driving in the dark was perilous. I had scratched my new car coming out of the car park. Shaking and apologizing to my car, I slowly made my way to the restaurant. When I mentioned the incident to my students, Shanti volunteered to drive me home whenever it got dark early, and later on Les came to the rescue and would take me back and forth to Gibraltar every Wednesday.

The following day Lucy, a student from Portugal, drove all the way to my home in Spain, to see me. As I only had a one-bedroom apartment she slept on the sofa in the lounge, and during the day she helped me sort out all my technical issues and DIY jobs. She came, took over what needed to be done and left after a couple of days expecting nothing in return. Two other friends, Ole and Kim, came frequently to see me to make sure I was okay. I felt incredibly blessed.

Shortly afterwards I received a package by DHL from my good friend, Marina, in Barcelona and when I opened it, it was an air ticket to Marrakesh and confirmation of a booking at a luxury spa hotel. I gasped! How did she know? During our marriage I had asked Shanky to take me to Marrakesh many times but we never managed it. After he passed I was going through his computer, and I discovered he had been researching hotels in Marrakesh. It looked as though he was going to take me there after all! You can imagine how I felt when I received the package. I called Marina immediately to thank her for such an extraordinary gift and asked, "Marina, why did you choose Marrakesh?"

"I don't know. I passed this travel agency and saw it advertised and thought to myself that is where I will take Nalanie to cheer her up and she can have a break. You have given me spiritual knowledge and I am so grateful for that. This is my thank you."

That trip to Morocco was truly special. I cried, I laughed and enjoyed both the pain and pleasure with my good friend Marina. I was sure that Shanky had telepathically placed the thought of Marrakesh into her mind.

Family and friends lighten the path of pain when we let them in and accept their love as a gift. To be humble and truthful to one's self brings us all the support we need. I felt my Shanky was always with me and was carrying me through it.

That whole first year was filled with so many things, and not all of them cathartic. I was fortunate to be able to travel and undertook several speaking engagements, and revisit some of the charitable projects that were begun before Shanky's passing. Travel took my mind off the pain and I felt I still had a purpose. Though the pain was still there, throbbing and gnawing away, it was gradually becoming more bearable, and travel provided a welcome respite.

But the year also held in store yet more tragedy.

In February I received word that Vijay had lost his battle with cancer and had left his physical body. I did not have the energy to attend his funeral. My sister Kantu totally understood. She did not have the strength to have so many family members visiting.

Then in May my family suffered the biggest and most terrible shock when my four-year-old nephew, Zubin, (Mira's grandson) died from meningitis. It was devastating news. I flew to Hong Kong in July to be with Mira, her husband Ramesh and their daughter Shalini, Zubin's mother, who was inconsolable.

During this time, I was also busy setting up the charity *'Service in Satchidananda'* in Spain. The idea was to formalize what I had practised for years and, in honour of Swami Satchidananda, to advance the doctrine of Karma Yoga, of service to the community and to humanity without expecting anything in return. In promoting this new charity, I visited several places such as Estoril in Portugal, where I gave my first *satsang* since Shanky left his body, to a small group of people in the home of my good friend Ulla Rapazote. I used this *satsang* to convey my experiences over the previous few months and how I was slowly coming to terms with the loss of my husband. Naturally, just as it had been when I first spoke at the Gibraltar centre, it was extremely difficult for me and I had to struggle to hold back the tears. But at the same time, talking so openly about the pain somehow helped me to heal. A gentleman came up to me after that talk and commented, "I wish I had met you five years ago when I first lost my wife. I have been stuck in sorrow for five years. Feelings of guilt, self-blame, anger and frustration have enveloped me all these years. After hearing you speak with such acceptance only three months after your husband's passing, has encouraged me to start living again. I am useful and I am now tired of wallowing in self-pity."

I closed my eyes and whispered, *'Shanky, thank you for helping this gentleman. Yes. This is what I am meant to do. Lift hearts and give hope.'*

May of that year was a turning point for me. I was teaching an intensive residential course in Raja Yoga at a retreat centre called *Quinta da Calma* in the Algarve, Portugal. It lasted seventeen days and I had seventeen participants. I have taught this course many times over the years. This time was very different. This time I was different.

Over my many years of practice, I had witnessed the amazing power that emanates from studying the *Yoga Sutras of Patanjali*. It had transformed my life, and many more lives, from drudgery to joy and understanding.

What then is Raja Yoga? And who was Patanjali? It is estimated that he (or it could have been a group of people using the same title) lived over three thousand years ago. The fact is, nobody truly knows.

The word 'sutra' means thread. Sutras are threads of knowledge. The knowledge of who we truly are; how to get to that place of peace, and in doing so live out our life's purpose. Our vision changes from a personal egotistic view of life to one that expands our consciousness to the awareness that we are truly one universal family.

Raja Yoga focuses on what is called 'the eight limbs of Yoga'. The first two, *Yama* and *Niyama*, are rather like the Ten Commandments or Buddha's eight-fold path to Nirvana. By observing these spiritual laws we enhance our lives and the lives of others too. The teaching is that what we toss out to the world is what we will receive from it. It is the law of the universe that 'every action has an equal and opposite reaction'. In other words, it is the law of Karma.

The *Yamas* list out the importance of being non-violent, and of being truthful not only to others but especially to ourselves. They further advise that stealing and over consumption, lust, addictions and greed lead us to a place of 'dis-ease' and bear unfavourable consequences.

The *Niyamas* point out that the practice of purity of thoughts and looking after our body will help us in our endeavours in this world. They teach us that the practice of contentment leads us to a place of supreme peace; that accepting pain is part of life's process, and bitterness and anger only serve to make us more miserable. Further, we are taught that the study of uplifting and spiritual books helps to reinforce our practice and takes us to a place of true understanding of spirit. In the words of Wayne Dyer, 'We are spiritual beings having a human experience'. And, finally, the *Niyamas* state that we should 'surrender to Ishvara'. *Ishvara* refers to the Higher Self however one chooses to see it, for example, God or Consciousness.

The third limb of Yoga explains how important *Asana* is. It entails looking after our bodies through Hatha Yoga practices, or by exercising. It is essential for our body to remain fit in order to be able to live a good life. The importance of diet is also mentioned.

The fourth limb is *Pranayama*, the practice of breath control, which oxygenates the entire system and has amazing effects on quieting the mind. *Pratyahara*, the fifth limb, talks about sense control; in other words, we learn to be aware of our senses rather than allow them to overtake and control us.

The sixth limb, *Dharana*, is the practice of concentration, which leads on to the seventh limb, *Dhyana*, meaning 'meditation'. Meditation connects us to our higher Self and enables us to witness our thoughts and see them, as one would observe clouds floating by. One minute there and the next minute, gone. What you can see, you can change. If the mind is full of negative thoughts, we can change them by focusing on opposite positive thoughts, in effect rewiring the brain. I often liken it to having a virus on the computer and removing the virus by introducing a new program.

When the mind becomes still and neutral, we then experience the eighth and last limb of Yoga, a state of *Samadhi*, or absolute bliss. The Buddhists call this state "Nirvana".

When I first embarked on this path, through the grace of my wonderful Gurudeva, I was rather lost, saddened by the state of the world, and really could not fathom what life was all about. What I learnt from the spiritual study was that all life is a great masterpiece and my part, albeit tiny, could influence the vibration around me and within me. The study took me from my little world of self-importance to a world beyond myself. I realized the cause of my illness was the fact that I felt victimized and disillusioned by the world. I was born an asthmatic. As I grew older, my health deteriorated. I developed eczema and ulcers, which only worsened the asthmatic attacks. With the practice of meditation, and after only six months, I noticed my intake of medicines had gradually reduced by half. As my approach to life changed, my health improved rapidly. This exhilarated me! Not only that, I was overcome by so many fears at that time but then, over the years, with the realization of the Higher Self these fears slowly started to leave me. I felt then, that I had to share this experience with others.

Literally, I changed my mind and my life transformed before me. I started to work as a counsellor dealing with all kinds of problems that people encountered: bereavement, addictions, sicknesses, special needs, to list just a few, and I witnessed how this great science helped and served them. The secret was to empower people by giving them the tools so that they could heal themselves. I saw what limited us was our belief systems. When we alter our mind-sets to the abundance of the universe, no matter how hard a situation, it always provides us with a solution, perhaps not the one we wished for but certainly one that was better for us. I started to see the perfect pattern of creation. What joy! What freedom! It was through the self-discipline of daily practice of these eight limbs of Yoga that the truth unfolded before my eyes. And it is so true; 'as we sow, we shall reap'.

I was not sure how I would react during that intensive Raja Yoga course in Portugal. Was I up to teaching eight hours daily with the heaviness I felt in my heart? I surprised myself by thoroughly loving the time with the students. Teaching this great 'science of the mind' jerked me back into the present and to the memory that all life is an illusion, what we call *maya* in Sanskrit. What do I mean by that? In the Yoga Sutras of Patanjali, it is explained that ignorance is the primary cause for suffering.

'Ignorance is regarding the impermanent as the permanent, impure as the pure, the painful as pleasant, and the non-Self as the Self.'
(Yoga Sutras of Patanjali. Book 2, Sutra 5)

I was once again reminded that all life was transient and everything would pass including the sorrow. At that moment, the others needed me to pass the knowledge I had gained throughout my life's experiences. My responsibility was to give the best of myself.

Over those precious days I witnessed the students move from weakness to strength, from anger to forgiveness, from sorrow to joy, from selfishness to selflessness. As I observed the transformation in them, I saw the transformation in me. Yes, service was truly a healer.

In June of that year, I travelled to Nepal where the Integral Yoga Centre charity had bought land on which to build a school in a village called Meghauli situated in the south of the country. We liaised with a wonderful gentleman by the name of Hari Bhandary. His story is a remarkable one. He was born to a poor family living in this tiny village. One day, as a young man, he rescued some foreign tourists who were lost and escorted them back to safety. They never forgot his kindness and as a token of their appreciation they paid for Hari to attend school in Kathmandu. Seeing and experiencing first hand the plight of the poor in Nepal, Hari decided he would dedicate his life to improving the living conditions of his fellow villagers and of his family. Whatever money he earned was shared and distributed amongst the villagers. His passion, sincerity and humility won the hearts of many visiting foreigners some of whom decided to fund Hari's dream of bringing sanitation, education and medicine to Meghauli. One of the donors to Hari's cause resided in Gibraltar and invited him there. During his visit a member of our *sangha* introduced Hari to us at our Centre and I immediately intuited that we needed to raise funds to help this humble, gentle soul. We then proceeded to raise a not insignificant sum of money and we were able to purchase the land on which to build the much needed school. I was fortunate to be able to fly to Nepal in order to visit the site and begin negotiations for its acquisition.

And now I found myself flying back to Nepal to view the architect's drawings, to meet a woman from the United States whom Hari had met and, so he informed us, would be the perfect candidate for running the school. Marina had decided to join us in this endeavour along with two of her colleagues from her charity *Vida Util*. Les, the member of the Gibraltar and Spain *sanghas*, had recently separated from his wife, so he also came along to help out. In 2003 Les started his own charity called *The Association for Kids In Need* - or 'AKIN' for short - which he established out of the desire to make a difference in the world by educating poor children and orphans living in the so-called 'third world' countries through sponsorships and donations. I held him in high esteem, having worked with him when he spearheaded the establishment of a telephone helpline service in Gibraltar, called *Childline Gibraltar*, to protect abused children. Little did I suspect at the time that the gods had planned something more for us!

That trip to Nepal was extraordinary. We planted a tree on the land we had purchased in honour of Shanky and then performed a *puja* - a Hindu prayer ceremony - to inaugurate the land and derive blessings from God. We visited the kindergarten school and the orphanage we had raised money to support, and the clean water taps and latrines that we had paid to be installed in the vicinity. The mortality rate amongst the poor Nepalese children in that area was drastically reduced as a result of these new facilities. How good it made us all feel! We stayed in Hari's home enjoying the delicious cuisine that his family laid out for us. We sang mantras with the villagers and went to sleep surrounded by all manner of bugs! There were insects everywhere of all different shapes, colours and sizes, and Marina and I would draw the sheets over our heads to avoid being bitten. Space in Hari's home was limited so Marina and I shared a room and giggled like children, and I felt the joy creeping back into my life.

Marina, Hari, Les and myself developed a deep friendship during this time. We delved deep into spiritual issues and shared our personal experiences.

Before Shanky passed he was adamant that I should not go back to Nepal. He was convinced I would be infected by a deadly disease. I was allergic to many drugs so I refused to take any inoculations before I travelled but instead boosted myself up with vitamins. It was obvious that had he lived, I would not have travelled to Nepal. At the time, though, it was apparent this work was necessary, in fact it was vital not just for the people of Meghauli but also for me, so that I could heal. Sadly, however, the school project fell apart a year and a half later. For some inexplicable reason, still unknown to this day, the person who Hari thought was the perfect candidate to run the school, sabotaged the whole project. I was saddened by this turn of events but, at the same time, I had to smile because I knew Shanky was protecting me from something worse. The funds we raised were diverted to refurbishing the orphanage, which was in desperate need of it.

Following Shanky's passing I received quite a few blows from people I totally trusted and loved. But after enduring the pain of losing him, everything else faded into the background. And again I heard the same words in my mind, 'the Divine plan is perfect. Everything works for the best. With patience you will get all the answers, Nalanie'. I had learned to trust that inner voice, and I understood that all the betrayals I endured were tests for my soul. The art of forgiving and letting go was maturing in me. I call it my 'flourishing into Spirit' time.

I subsequently returned to Nepal, just one more time. With Les and Marina. It was following the 2016 earthquake that devastated the country. We had collected funds to rebuild four houses lost in the earthquake, and in doing so help to rebuild the lives of some of the victims. I was then extremely blessed to be able to fulfil a lifelong dream - to visit Bhutan. This tiny yet incredibly beautiful country is so peaceful, so spiritual. A delight, and food for my soul.

Once more, life became a beautiful canvas. It is up to each individual to paint their picture the best they can. Small canvas or big canvas, it does not matter. The joy of producing a painting is the fun of it. We should all paint beautiful pictures to enhance the splendour of our world.

Chapter 5
Family Matters

Mom and Dad

My mother was never the same after the demise of my father in 2006, two years before Shanky left his body. She was angry for a long time and slowly detached herself emotionally from everything. After my father's funeral she said to me, "I have not only lost my husband, I have lost my Guru, my Parmeshwara (God). What is left for me now?"

My father was a saintly man. As a child I used to pray that I would be so grateful to God if I could be just a small percentage of what he was. He was the embodiment of pure love. He worked himself up from rags to riches and never forgot his humble beginnings. He served the poor and needy not only at home in Hong Kong but all over the globe. He was a man of integrity and responsibility, firm in his belief that his birth as the eldest son of eight children was his God given privilege of looking after them all. He was generosity personified to everyone who crossed his path. He explained to me that whenever anyone came to him for help, it was God that had sent them. He constantly told us, his children, *'Give love, give love. Only by giving love will you get love.'* He took us everywhere with him when he travelled and it is through him, I learnt much about the world and humanity. He took us to the finest of places and to the poorest of places. He educated us to the power of God and how important it was to be grateful daily. He taught us God was everywhere and in everyone, irrelevant of religion, race or caste. He was called 'Dada' - a Hindu term of respect - by all and was the community's spiritual and business advisor, arbitrator and confidant. I could write an entire book about my father, and so could all my and his siblings.

When he passed, my whole family grieved tremendously. I was deeply saddened but at the same time I was relieved for him. He had been suffering from cancer for many years. He never complained about his pain. He told me he was ready to leave the earth, as his body was no longer functioning properly, and he was only staying because he had promised my Mom they would celebrate their 60th wedding anniversary before he would depart.

Mom would freeze and become very upset every time he spoke of death so he stopped talking about it with her, but when I visited them for their 60th anniversary he confided to me he was happy he could talk to me freely, as I understood we were soul and that we never died. He was not afraid of leaving this world at all. He only wanted all the family to be ready for his departure. I felt honoured that my father confided in me, that he felt comfortable he could talk about death without me freaking out. He asked me to write a letter for him stating that he did not want Mom to wear white for the rest of her life after he left. Indian custom dictates a widow wears white clothes after the husband's passing. He wanted her to wear colourful clothing and all the jewellery he had bought her. Then he signed it and asked me to show it to my uncle Hari and to tell him to notify my Mom of his wishes. Mom respected my uncle and would listen to him.

Dad died at 86 years. What a life he led! He travelled the world, met with royalty, met with paupers, served, loved, gave and was revered. How could I be sad for him? However, I did miss his presence in this world tremendously. Dad was my security blanket and my mentor. Again, I was grateful that the practice of Yoga had prepared me for this loss. *'Our loss; heaven's gain.'* He articulated many times that heaven and hell existed on this earth. After this world there was only love. I took great comfort in those words and they remain my belief system to this day.

Mom, on the other hand, is a traditionalist. She is a devout Hindu woman and her faith in God is unshakeable. She was a 'super-mom' in that she loved us all and cared for us. However, she was extremely strict and we, her children, being brought up in Hong Kong, frequently rebelled and in consequence incurred and bore her anger, which could be frightening. She really had a challenging time raising seven of us children! It is odd how we all understood it was not her fault she was so strict. We knew her upbringing had been quite tough and that she was given no freedom as a child. Dad was the first man she was allowed to meet outside her family. Her marriage was arranged after having met him for only half an hour.

After Dad's demise she developed dementia. She resorted to prayer and till today she is constantly praying. We are grateful for this, as we see she is truly peaceful in her world. From time to time when we visit her she will become lucid and recollect certain memories. She even remembers how much she loves us! Most of the time she is detached and serene. Through her I learnt that there was a vast difference between being religious and being spiritual.

I arrived in Hong Kong in April with my granddaughter Natasha accompanying me. My son Shaman picked us up from the airport and my heart leaped with joy. To receive his strong hug meant so much to me. When I arrived at the family home, where I had grown up and was going to stay, I found Mom lying down in her room unable to face me. I understood immediately it wasn't that she did not want to, she just did not have the strength to deal with my loss. I walked up to the bed and said, "Mom, I heard you have a bad headache. Mom, now that I have lost Shanky, I understand your sorrow. I know how much you must miss Dad. Please do not worry about me. I am strong."

I gave her a kiss on the cheek and went to the sitting room to have a cup of coffee with my son and Hersha who had arrived with Indira. Five minutes later, my Mom appeared refreshed.

"Nal, I come to have tea with you, have a biscuit, eat something, you come from long flight. I am better now." My Mom's command of English was not that good. After that there was no mention of my husband's death nor did she ever ask how I was managing. My sister Mira was upset at Mom. She felt for me. I told Mira to let the anger go, as I truly wasn't dismayed by Mom's reaction. I explained how, after going through such pain myself, I totally comprehended Mom's disposition. I loved and adored my Mom and frankly did not want her to suffer on my behalf.

Mira

From Nepal, I again flew to Hong Kong, this time to be with my sister Mira and her husband Ramesh, and her family after the passing of her grandson, Zubin. I empathized with their heartbreak even though on the face of it they seemed resilient. My sister was a philanthropist. She spent her life serving the Indian community, organizing charity balls and producing plays to raise funds for those in need. Whenever there was a disaster somewhere in the world she would be up there, working tirelessly at the forefront of efforts to secure donations for the relief agencies. She was a supporter of Mother Teresa and raised vast sums of money for the *Missionaries of Charity* institution.

Mira was a marvellous sister to all us siblings. As the eldest of the seven, she was very protective especially towards her younger sisters. She was a second mom to me and after Shanky's death she constantly phoned and checked to see how I was doing. Now, I just wanted to support and comfort her family in their time of sorrow.

We talked about the suddenness of Zubin's death. The shock was immense. From having a stomach bug, it developed into influenza and in a matter of twenty-four hours he had died from meningitis. He was only four years old and such a gorgeous child. My niece Shalini, another humanitarian who fought for women's rights and the rights of ethnic minority groups, and her husband Ravi, were devastated. Shock, anger and disbelief overcame them and it took many years and much soul searching for them to recover some semblance of peace. They kept Zubin's name alive by setting up a charitable foundation in his honour and by celebrating his birthday every year with family and friends. My heart went out to them.

I asked my sister if she had allowed herself to fully grieve. I told her how important it was to cry and release the pain. I will never forget my sister's reply. She said, "Nal, you don't understand. If I cry, I won't stop and then I will get very sick. I cannot cry."

"Mira, there is so much grief buried in you and that is why it is essential you do shed those tears. You may get sick now but if you don't cry, you will be much worse later. In my line of work, I have observed that holding on to emotions blocks the energy flow in the body. And where there is no flow of energy, disease materializes. Please allow me to help you through this."

"No, Nal. You just lost Shanky. I cannot put you through any more sorrow. I am your elder sister and it is my responsibility to look after you."

But I was undeterred. "Sis, I really don't mind. I am strong and don't need protecting. At least allow me to do some creative visualization with you. We will get you to relax first, which will then allow the tears to flow easily and gently."

I asked her to lie down and once she had settled I put her into Yoga *nidra* (Yogic sleep or deep relaxation) using healing visualizations. She did not cry but she started burping a lot. I explained to her that burping was a sign of an emotional blockage in the digestive system that needed to be released, and that, as such, it was important to frequently repeat this method of treatment. Unfortunately, we lived in different continents and neither of us had much free time even though I visited Hong Kong often. It was Mira who organized public speaking engagements for me to talk about spiritual practices whenever I visited Hong Kong. And what a great organizer she was! She decorated the stage on which I sat so exquisitely and always made sure that I would have a large audience. I was very touched by her faith in me. Her daughter Minal is the one who does this for me now. She has become the embodiment of her mother.

My sister left the world in 2016. She was diagnosed with nasal pharyngeal cancer, in other words, cancer in the nasal passage (perhaps from a lack of tears leading to blocked ducts?) However, she did not die from the cancer but from a lung disease caused by an infection she had developed (a broken heart?) Blocked emotions can manifest in disease. I have seen this throughout my counselling career.

People deal with grieving in their own personal ways, and I would like to reiterate there is no right or wrong way. We are all individuals and we need to honour and respect this. Externally to the world, Mira was strong and carried on serving the community. Service and creativity were her survival tools. She carried the family's emotional state on her shoulders and was there for all of us, never thinking about herself. One time she attended a Raja Yoga Course I taught in Hong Kong, following which she told me it had changed her concept of things and she realized that it wasn't up to her to save everyone. Her contribution would be only to love them. I wish she had applied this love to herself.

When we believe that we can control life, people, things, circumstances, even emotions, if things don't work out the way we want, all that happens is we create stress within ourselves, become unhappy and eventually develop panic attacks. This sentiment imprisons us. All we can do is our best and realize certain things just are not under our control. When we let loose the tight reins of control, freedom becomes our gift. Freedom from desiring life to be the way we dictate it should. This want, this need, this 'I have to have' keeps us suffering. Whenever difficult situations surfaced in my life that made me want to control the circumstances, I would say this prayer and immediately let go.

> *Lord, grant me the serenity to accept the things I cannot change,*
> *The courage to change the things I can,*
> *And the wisdom to know the difference.*

It's taken years to rewire my mind but it has been definitely worth it!

Mira and I spent many hours discussing spiritual life. I miss her gentleness and kindness. She left me with one consolation. In our last conversation together before her demise, she voiced to me that she was not scared. She told me she had lived a wonderful life. She said she was just too tired and really did not want to go through chemotherapy. She hated the thought of radiation burning her face. She was ready to leave and join Dad and the others in our family who had departed this life. She got her wish; she never had to endure chemotherapy or radiotherapy, as she developed pneumonia.

A few months before her passing she gave me a book entitled *Being Mortal: Medicine and What Matters in the End* by American surgeon Atul Gawande. She insisted I read it quickly. The book was about how unsympathetic the medical system can be in denying people the right to choose the way they wanted to die. Old people were often kept alive with machines, all their independence stripped away and treated as though they did not have a voice. It challenged all of us to look at palliative care as a better alternative or, if one can afford it, to allow the elderly to die in their homes with the support of nurses and carers. Mira's soul knew her time was close and she wanted me to know her wishes, which she relayed to her family and made them promise they would adhere to her terms. They were upset with her for voicing this, except for her youngest daughter Minal. She told me Minal was her 'Florence Nightingale' and that in her presence she could express her sentiments without getting a barrage of opinions. The others felt Mira was selfish to want to leave. In the end Mira did agree to go through chemotherapy and radiotherapy. The thought of it stressed her out a lot but, being Mira, she just could not be selfish. The Universe heard her wishes and she got her way in the end.

This difference of opinions often occurs in families, each one thinking they know best. I frequently suggest to families to listen to what the sick person is trying to tell them and then gently give their opinion without making anyone feel guilty. Emotions run high because of fear. Fear of the loss of a loved one. The last thing the sick person needs to hear is all the debate and anger. They already have a lot to deal with physically, emotionally and spiritually. This lesson Shanky taught me well.

When Mira was nearing the end of her life, all us siblings flew to Hong Kong and surrounded her with love. We went to the hospital every day, some for long hours. Her children and husband went beyond the call of duty to make everything so easy and comfortable for her. There were many tears at her funeral. Many loved her and voiced their gratitude for having known her. After she passed, her supporters, family and friends held a charity ball in her name and every single ticket was sold out within hours. She lived a fulfilled life and during her last hours on earth she was surrounded by family singing mantras and pouring all their love upon her. We all said our goodbyes gently and lovingly. She lived and died beautifully.

--oOo--

So much happened that first year following Shanky's passing. After Hong Kong, I went back to Spain and continued with the weekly classes there and in Gibraltar. I continued with spiritual counselling, travelling and teaching. Whatever free time I had I spent with Shani, Andrew and the grandchildren. Tara and Natasha stayed many weekends at my apartment and truly lifted my spirits more than anything else did. They constantly asked me for 'Yoga Stories' (stories with morals) and I would fall asleep telling them, which would make them giggle! On weekday evenings, I would take long walks by the beach, watching the waves crash against the shore. Memories of our thirty-four years together would flood in. Good times, bad times all gone. All passed. A dream. But, one thing did not go. The love in my heart, and gratitude for a life together, my life with this dynamic soul who could be so frustrating at times! And I smiled at his presence in my heart, as I knew he always heard me.

I recall the words of my Spiritual Master from long ago when he asked me when I would visit him at the ashram in Virginia. I answered, "Gurudev, I do not know. I have so much work at the shop. My husband and children need me."

He asked me, "Nalanie, how many waves crash against the shore?"

I looked at him quizzically and answered, "An infinite amount, they never stop."

"When will you spend time with your soul and find the Divine Source?" he replied. "Life never stops. Today it's your husband, then your children, then it's Christmas, then the children graduate, then they marry, then you have grandchildren. And one day you will die. It will never stop. Excuses are infinite."

After that I booked to go to the ashram. A powerful lesson was given to me. 'Never put off till tomorrow what you can achieve today. Time waits for no one.' I am grateful I listened to that advice.

Kantu

I went to visit my sister Kantu in New Jersey that December with Bhavani, one of our sangha members. She was still broken and refused to listen to any of the music she and Vijay loved. So, one evening, Bhavani and I placed Kantu between us on the sofa and turned on all their favourite songs. Together, we cried, laughed, danced and watched Kantu's energy becoming lighter and lighter. We then looked through some photographs, the graphic memories of her life with Vijay. She cried a lot, and I was grateful that I was there to hug her and show her that it was possible to feel peace in the pain.

Kantu had two sons but at the time they were both away in University. She lived in a large house and it was only after she sold her home and moved into smaller accommodation that she finally started her road to healing. After Vijay passed our brother David, his wife Avisha and Mira had all been wonderful to her. They travelled to the States and helped her organize all the official paperwork. And then there was Junior, a Godsend. Junior had worked with Vijay for over thirty years and had promised Vijay he would look after Kantu. He kept his promise and became like a father to her. Family and close friends are vital at this time. Vijay leaving her had created a huge void. Kantu was a wonderful housewife and spent her life serving her family, which was highly admirable. She and Vijay had a close group of friends they went out with once in a while. Now suddenly he was gone and the boys were at university. The days seemed so long and lonely for Kantu. My heart went out to her. I realized how blessed I was that I had always worked and was passionate about teaching Yoga. It kept my 'monkey mind' busy with healthy thoughts. Kantu and I had long talks about her finding herself. I was relieved to learn she had decided to travel to Hong Kong and stay with the family there for a few months. She had many friends in Hong Kong and I knew our family would give her the love she needed to heal. My advice to those grieving is, make sure you spend time with friends. When you lose a spouse and your children live away, loneliness can make it doubly hard. There is an emptiness that friends can help to fill.

It was difficult for me to leave her and return to Spain.

--oOo--

I was dreading the 23rd of December. A year since Shanky's passing. Shani, Andrew and the children all came to my apartment and we performed a *puja* for him. Andrew drank whisky and ate Spanish ham in honour of Shanky who loved those things. We embraced each other. What to do? *It is as it is*, I told my family. I refused to let the sadness and pain prevent me from celebrating Christmas with the children. Christmas was always a very special time for our family. On Christmas Eve we would all get together for dinner. Shanky would cook some lamb and I would cook the vegetables. We always had a laugh and an amazing time.

My daughter looked at me and said, "Mom, this year you are coming to our home. I have invited our friends Haresh and Anju and their children to join us, as they have done all these years. I will ask Les as well, as he is alone. We will celebrate Christmas Eve as we always have. Dad would want that. Please allow me to do this for you."

I nodded with gratitude. We would miss Shaman, Hersha and Indira but that was okay, as they were with all the family in Hong Kong. I knew they would find it hard, but they would be fine. My son was blessed with a loving wife.

I was glad when the year was over. Three family deaths and three betrayals. My brother Maj still undergoing treatment for his cancer. Talia constantly in-and-out of hospital. And Les, who had become a dear friend, had been diagnosed with a rare form of bone cancer.

Yet, despite all this, I felt protected with all the love that surrounded me. My Yoga students were all so kind. They felt they needed my service and that gave me motivation and purpose.

Yes, I had acquired the three ingredients that I needed to help me heal: To be easeful, peaceful and useful.

A New Year and a new beginning were dawning.

Chapter 6
Acceptance And Letting Go

New Beginnings

'The pain of loss is forever in my heart,
The grace of God is forever by my side,
The night and day speak out his name,
They tell me things on earth will never be the same.
The colours and sounds call out to me,
And promise moments of joy and peace.
My love has left his human form,
No more can I touch those hands and feel the warmth.
My soul torn into two - half here, half there.
Nalanie, there's no need to despair.
My spirit soars at his gain.
He is where there is no pain.
Spirit to spirit we can touch with Love.
And that's where we are always one.

This poem was an entry in my diary towards the end of 2009. My life was filled with meaning, but I wasn't fully embracing it. There was much to look forward to with many charitable projects coming my way. Yet, in the background there was a heart still dull with pain. Time, I continuously repeated to myself. One day the throbbing will disappear.

I was my own doctor and this empowered me. Acceptance was the key to recovery. Acceptance of the pain I was enduring, acceptance of situations that did not work out the way I thought they would, acceptance of what each person's version of grieving was, acceptance that there was nobody to blame, and acceptance of life in general. This world is a University and not all lessons are easy.

Surrendering came soon after acceptance. I surrendered in humility to the great force called 'God' and remembered my father's words: *'You are never alone, God is always with you, in your very own heart. All you have to do is give love.'*

I would like to relate a story that I often use in my lectures whenever I speak about acceptance and surrender.

There was a farmer called Lee who lived in a small village in China with his wife and son. His greatest possession besides his family was a horse. One day his neighbour, whose dream was to own a horse, went to him and said, "You are so lucky to own a horse."

Lee answered, "Good luck, bad luck, who knows?"

A few days later, the horse sprinted away and they could not retrieve it. The neighbour ran to Lee's home and said, "What bad luck that your only horse should run away."

Lee answered, "Good luck, bad luck, who knows?"

A few days later the horse returned followed by two stallions. The neighbour saw them arrive and went immediately to see Lee and said, "You must be the luckiest man I know. Your horse ran away and has returned with two beautiful stallions!"

Lee answered, "Good luck, bad luck, who knows?"

Lee's son decided to train one of the stallions and was thrown off the horse and onto the ground. He sustained heavy injuries. The neighbour said to Lee, "I thought you were lucky but now I can see that you really are not! Look at your son, it will take some time before he can walk again."

Lee answered, "Good luck, bad luck, who knows?"

At that time there was a war being waged in China and the next day the Emperor's representatives arrived in the village to conscript young men into the army. Because Lee's son was badly injured they couldn't use him, but the neighbour's son was healthy so he was led away to fight in the war. The neighbour arrived at Lee's home with tears in his eyes and said, "You are truly lucky, you have your son at home with you. I may never see my son again."

Lee answered, "Good luck, bad luck, who knows?"

The story describes the way I look at life. I am grateful for each moment and my main focus is on being in the 'now', what Swami Satchidananda called 'The Golden Present'. He taught me the profound lesson that nothing is permanent. The only constant is change. And I saw a change in myself. I became less sensitive and I began to regard life as one great show; well, maybe not so great sometimes! 'Good luck, bad luck, who knows?'

I started the New Year with renewed energy although I must admit my memory was still not a hundred per cent. This is one thing I noticed in many of the people I have counselled who have suffered loss. Bereavement affects the memory and many become anxious, as they think dementia has begun to set in. I allay their fears by telling them my own story and explaining it is all part of the grieving process.

When you lose someone close, especially if the loss is sudden, the mind goes through several phases. Initially there is disbelief and even denial, which sends the mind into a dark place where seemingly unconnected or half completed thoughts race out of control and draw you deeper and deeper into yourself as you search for meaning, search for answers. This state draws you away from the real world, and situations that you would normally give your full attention to are no longer so important. People speak to you but only a few of their words remain with you, to be forgotten in the mist that has become your mind. Self absorption temporarily removes you from what is going on around you, and even affects the memory so that something that ordinarily takes no effort to recall suddenly requires effort, requires you to come out of the confused mire that your thought processes have become and to focus. But it's normal. In such circumstances memory loss is temporary, and over time, as the pain eases, the mind regains its focus. You just need to understand and accept it. This, too, shall pass.

As I mentioned earlier, one project I immediately threw myself into was setting up the charity 'SIS', which stands for 'Service in Satchidananda', in honour of our Master. I would like to say more about this project because so many good things happened following the decision to form it that reinforced my belief and my faith in both the Divine and in humanity. I have long understood and accepted that good things happen if you just 'go with the flow', if you accept, if you 'do your best and let God do the rest.'

One day Gurudeva's former secretary, Prem Anjali, called me from the Ashram in Virginia and asked if we could offer one hundred good deeds in Gurudeva's name in time for the one hundredth anniversary of his birth, which would be in December 2012. I loved the idea, so we steamed ahead. Almost immediately we formed a great team of volunteers including Shanti Alman, who kindly offered to be my PA, Lucy 'Luckshmi' Cannon and Ulla Rapazote in Portugal, Marina Nadal in Barcelona, and Les Roberts in Gibraltar. Everything flowed. My Spanish lawyer, Nuria Agostin, introduced me to a friend of hers by the name of Jesus Nunoz, who specialized in setting up charities. Jesus arranged the registration of SIS in Spain and took care of all the official paperwork, and he refused to charge me a penny. I had never met Jesus before, but after only meeting me for half an hour he announced his services would be his gift to humanity! I could clearly see the Divine hand in this, and it was not the only occasion when Divine Providence stepped in to move things along! Les, who worked as a company secretary and compliance officer, drafted our vision and mission statements along with the objects of the charity, and Amber Turner, a friend who was a Gibraltar-based lawyer and *sangha* member, assisted me by attending the meetings I held with Jesus. As a team, we were on fire and even decided to establish a branch of the charity called 'Little Miracles' that would be devoted to the service of children with special needs.

Everything about SIS just flowed, and we flowed with it. Random acts of kindness - the good deeds we promised our Master - started happening in Gibraltar, in Spain, in Portugal, in the US, in the United Kingdom, in Finland, in Hong Kong, and everywhere! When we needed donations, for example, to help feed or provide medicines to the poor, the money would flow in. Not only did we accomplish the objective of offering one hundred good deeds by December 2012 but the number of selfless acts of service continued to rise and rise, and continues to this day.

Our objective was and remains very simple. To give help wherever it is needed. And the 'Little Miracles' initiative was naturally inspired by my own experiences with my very special granddaughter, Talia. By observing Talia's struggle and her progress, knowledge was gained that proved useful so that SIS could also help children like her. Inadvertently, in a way, Talia became part of the team and I was convinced her soul chose a broken body and came to our family so that we could learn and make a difference to the lives of children with special needs.

My daughter, Shani, was too busy helping Andrew with their real estate business, looking after the girls and searching for a diagnosis for Talia. She would help us whenever she could, and I helped her whenever I could. I travelled with her to several medical conferences and learnt much about different debilitating conditions and illnesses. Going to Talia's sessions with Ana, her physiotherapist, increased my knowledge and witnessing Ana's expertise enhanced my own work with children. Talia started to thrive with Ana who engaged Talia with her energy and determination. There was a bond between therapist and patient. Talia wanted to please Ana, and Ana was unwavering in her belief that Talia would walk.

I began working with special needs children when I was just 12 years old. Every Saturday I would volunteer to go to the centre for children with special needs in Hong Kong with the nuns from my school. Back then, those precious children were treated so badly. Some were tied to their beds because there were not enough carers or helpers to deal with them. I remember crying and telling the nuns that it was all so wrong. The nuns explained that these children were lucky to be in a home, as many parents wanted nothing to do with their disabled children and abandoned them.

I have always been drawn towards children with special needs, and when Talia was born my soul intuited that she, my beautiful granddaughter, would play a major role in my life. It is because of her that I have met some incredibly wonderful disabled people who became some of my greatest teachers. I sometimes wonder with whom the real disability lies. These children's souls seem much purer than many of us. I admire some of their parents, as it is in them that I have seen the greatest selfless service. I have met many 'real Yogis' who walked their talk, and through them I came to realize that Yoga is far greater than what I had been teaching. My understanding deepened. Yoga is not about teaching. It is about living a beautiful life in connection with the highest good.

Whenever people suggest that the world is terrifying and worse than it has ever been, I always disagree with them and use the example of how disabled children are treated today. There is now so much more available for them than ever before. In addition, there is now a vast amount of research being carried out into possible causes encompassing genetics and DNA. Fast forward a few years and I am sure many syndromes will be either avoidable or curable.

To counter any suggestion that the state of the world is worse than at any time in history I would also mention that globally, if we look at women's rights, things have changed dramatically. It is only a hundred years ago that women won the right to vote! Only a hundred years - and now look at women! We have fought hard for our rights to be respected and heard, and we are living in a generation where this is finally happening. The world *IS* becoming better and we need to endorse that sentiment. Remember: As we think, so it becomes. Fear attracts negative scenarios and faith brings about favourable ones.

So many of the people I have counselled came to see me because they were filled with fear. Fear of the state of the world, fear of the unknown, fear of not being good enough, fear of not achieving their goals, fear of being disliked, fear of failure, fear of the dark, fear of heights and other phobias, fear of being alone, fear of sickness, death and, in particular, the fear of being alive with these fears! And many more anxieties, ranging in complexity and severity. I recognized myself in all of them, having gone through most of these fears myself at some point in my life. Yet, through the practice of Yogic techniques I was able to watch myself heal from most of them, slowly but surely. My own experience gave me the answers to many of their problems.

I always feel such joy when their faces light up at the end of the sessions. When I see hope, strength and energy, a life force, re-enter their lives my heart sings, and that is my greatest reward. For what is life without hope? I have always worked on a donation basis with all donations going towards our charity. It was my job to make sure we constantly had enough money to look after the people we had made promises to help. At the end of a consultation I would frequently be asked how much I charged. I always answered, "If this session has helped you then please share the knowledge you have gained to help someone else so that we can keep the energy of love and service rolling. If you want to leave a donation, it will go straight towards the charity."

I loved to see the bewilderment on their faces. "Are you sure?"

When I answered in the affirmative, I could almost hear them think, *'now I really want to get better!'*

This is the way I still work. People have been so generous and whenever we have required urgent funds to support anyone in need, the *sangha* members have always stepped up and collected whatever was needed. We have always operated an open book policy so that anyone who enquires can see exactly where the money goes and how much we have in the bank accounts, which is never very much, as my rule is that whatever monies are donated to the charity should immediately be put to good use, to serve wherever or whoever has a need. Working this way has made life so simple for me and for my team all of whom are volunteers. To have a team of people work for the highest good and with no expectations is rare to find in this world. There is not a day goes by when I do not thank the universe for them. To be surrounded by beautiful souls with such pure hearts filled with love has given me the impetus to keep working and serving.

For me truth is of utmost importance. If I sense that a client is not benefiting from the methods I use, I suggest they see someone else who may be better equipped to help them with their problems. I have met and come to know many great healers in my life. There is so much out there now with a vast array of alternative remedies. It is often the case that clients need additional help from other sources such as massage therapy, kinesiology, homeopathy, naturopathy, Ayurveda, diet and nutrition to name a few. Some individuals may be lethargic due to a deficiency of certain supplements, and a change in diet and exercise can almost immediately alleviate their disposition.

Most people have referred to me as a 'soul doctor', which seems a fitting epithet! I like to introduce them to their souls, their true Selves. When their living patterns do not adhere to the laws of their spirit, dysfunction occurs. With the practice of Yoga, we can work inside-out or outside-in. Body, mind and spirit are all taken into consideration, as all components need to be addressed before healing can occur.

My prescription is simple:

Body:

First, I look at diet. I normally recommend a simple vegetarian diet so that the body takes less time to digest the food and more energy is available for healing. It is also important to drink enough water daily.

Then I teach them breathing techniques (pranayama) to alleviate stress. It may sound a little odd but many people do not know how to breathe properly. The correct technique can increase the flow of oxygen to the body up to seven times. These techniques also work brilliantly as a prerequisite for meditation. They help to still the mind.

Some form of physical exercise is also part of the process, so I suggest joining a Hatha Yoga Class or, if for any reason this is too much for them, I provide a sequence of postures for them to follow depending on their ability. Walking for at least 30 minutes every day and dancing and singing are also extremely therapeutic.

Mind:

Smile more! Laughter is the best medicine so I advise them to watch comedy shows on TV.

Distract the mind by adopting a new hobby, perhaps one they love but never got around to taking up, and devoting time to it at least once a week.

Self-analysis can be a great tool. People can get to know themselves better by listing their positive and negative qualities, and then help themselves by focussing on the positive qualities and starting to develop those more.

If the client is amenable to the idea I also recommend the study of spiritual books to be constantly reminded that our origin is Spirit or Soul or energy, however they wish to term it.

Practise gratitude constantly. I tell them that, whenever the mind travels to 'victimhood', it is vital to remind it of what you DO have and not what you don't. Be grateful for family and friends, for your home, for food, for whatever is good in your life and is often taken for granted. Many people focus on the negatives in their lives and go into 'why me?' mode, and in doing so they forget there is also so much that is positive and to be grateful for.

Selfless service is a fantastic healer! I ask them to think of at least one kind deed they can do every day. It doesn't have to be time consuming or complicated. It just needs to be kind. Simple acts of kindness can brighten the day for both the receiver and the giver.

To repeat positive affirmations daily with depth of feeling and emotion. By inputting the positive programming, we leave less space for the negative stories that spiral round and round in the mental realm. In Sanskrit this is called *pratipaksha bhavanam,* the replacing of a negative thought with an opposite positive one.

Finally, I give them a *mantra* that they feel comfortable with. The repetition of a phrase or saying over and over again helps to still the mind. A *mantra* can be anything. For a Christian it can be 'thy will be done'. For a Hindu, 'Om nama shivaya'. For an atheist it can be 'this too shall pass'.

Here is a simple drawing I came up with to demonstrate how changing the way we think can bring peace and joy.

Spirit:

The degree of understanding and acceptance of the final part of my prescription often depends on whether the individual believes in a deity or not, be it called *God* or *the Divine* or any other name or expression. I have found that most people believe in something but if there is doubt about or even rejection of the concept of spirit I ask them whether they believe in love or in peace. My Spiritual Master always said, "make peace your God" so I frequently use the word *peace,* as this is what everyone really wants in their lives and that is why those I counsel have come to see me. They are looking for peace and joy. It's just that they have temporarily forgotten that peace is their birthright because something has happened to disturb that peace.

Whether they are believers or not I strongly recommend they meditate for 15 minutes a day. Just sit still and breathe, be aware of one's breath. At first, if the mind is disturbed it is hard to focus, so it is best to start with 5 minutes and gradually increase as one becomes more comfortable. It is fashionable these days to have a figure of Buddha seated in meditation somewhere in the home (doubtless much to the chagrin of true Buddhists who consider Buddha much more than an ornament!) so the idea of meditation has become more acceptable. The benefits of meditation have also been widely documented and promoted, adding to its appeal.

For those who come from religious backgrounds I advocate sincere prayer. Not begging prayers but prayers for peace. If one has peace then one has everything. The difficult situations they find themselves in are a test of their faith. It is important to reinforce that faith and also to reinforce their belief in themselves.

Forgiveness of others, of situations and even forgiveness of oneself is vital on this journey. Guilt, anger, worry and obsessions mar the road to tranquillity. For this I give them a visualization that is personal to them to allow them to forgive and let go. If the hurt or anger is deep this process can take a long time. It may be hard but it is never impossible.

As Gurudev once said to me, *'the only thing we can do is to change what we do not like in ourselves. We are not here to change anyone; we do not have the right. We can advise them, but they are the only ones that can change themselves, if they want'.*

Whatever the problem or difficulty an individual may have gone through and that resulted in disturbing their peace, the probable cause is in the past and what is happening to them now is their reaction to it. Even if the traumatic situation is continuing, it is their reaction to it that is disturbing them. It is said *'the only constant is change'* so if all that is left of a difficult or traumatic situation is the victim's reaction to it, and even if the cause continues to disturb them the comforting message is the same: *This, too, shall pass.* In such situations it is helpful to practise being conscious of the present moment by focussing on the job at hand, and forgetting about the past. It has gone. And there is no point worrying about something in the future that may not happen. Our minds fret because we think, even believe, that something WILL happen, but, to quote the Yoga Sutras of Sri Patanjali, Book 2, Sutra 16: *'pain that is yet to come is avoidable'.* So allow joy to arise from the inner chamber of the heart by visualizing something that elevates. It can be a person, a memory, a scene, an object or anything that promotes peace and wellbeing.

I normally recommend books that will help them with this process. The more they practise, the sooner they get to their goals. And, again I turn to the Yoga Sutras of Patanjali and quote to them:

'Practice becomes firmly grounded when well attended to for a long time, without break and with all earnestness.' (Book 1, Sutra 14)

This actually is the perfect formula for anyone who wants to be successful in anything. The longer you work at something, the better at it you become on account of the continuous training and also your personal experiences. The secret is to love what you are doing. I often replace the word *earnestness* in the above quote with the word *love*. It has worked for me. I have loved and continue to love the work I am doing. I love the people who walk into my life no matter who they are. They feel this love. They feel it in the vibrational field as soon as they enter my space. Some are more receptive than others. I know it is this love that inspires them to love and care for themselves.

I tell my students that in life it is not possible to *like* everyone, but it is important to *love* everyone. How does one do this? By recognizing the 'Self', the consciousness that lives in all. *Namaste,* which means 'the Divine in me recognises the Divine in you', but at the same time understanding that the Divine is in everyone but not everyone is Divine! Judge the sin, not the sinner.

This is the way of the world we live in. A world of dualities and polarities. Where there is hate there is love. Where there is sorrow, there is joy; where there is right, there is wrong; where there is darkness, there is light. Everything in this phenomenal world has an opposite. The Yogi's journey is to transcend the opposites and observe every situation from a neutral standpoint. When we do this, we come to see there is truly no wrong or right. Just differences of opinions as each individual has their own set of experiences, which governs their thinking patterns. No two people are alike, we are all unique; we are all designer pieces. Our perception of life is determined by what we have encountered and experienced on life's journey. When undertaking his ecumenical work to bring people of all faiths and beliefs together, Sri Swami Satchidananda expounded that, 'Truth Is One, Paths Are Many'. This succinct axiom became the motto of the Integral Yoga Organisation he founded. There is only one Truth. How we find it is up to us.

The time I spend with each individual is always unique. I love to hear their stories and I ask them to narrate their life's circumstances to me as though they are writing their autobiography. How would they like the next chapter to read? We always have fun when we do this as possibilities of a happier life open up for them. There is an energy that pervades the room that is so powerful and benevolent. I know it comes from a higher source. I always pray for humility and to be a good instrument when these precious souls are placed in my energy field. I pray that they rediscover the joy and laughter in their lives.

'Did you know your birthright is to be happy? That is true spirituality. Real freedom is enjoying whatever you do'.

Swami Satchidananda.

Over the years I have been a counsellor I have been blessed to witness many people transforming their lives, and going on to live beautiful lives simply by knowing this one fundamental truth: *we are spirit, we are soul and the real Self 'with a capital S' never dies.*

I have also been extremely blessed to witness some wonderful events, which it would be easy to describe as 'miraculous'. But if you understand the one fundamental truth mentioned above then these same wonderful events can be seen as less miraculous, less inexplicable and mysterious. Whilst losing not one iota of their wonder they become the evidence to prove that one fundamental truth. It is said that 'faith is the evidence of things unseen' yet when the 'things unseen' become visible, faith is the natural consequence, reinforced and doubtless.

Two cases involving people I have counselled stand out. Both involve having faith in the higher power, in the Divine, in the Universe, in God. Whatever you wish to call it. The first is clear evidence that faith really works, and the second that, through faith, it is possible to let go of guilt and find peace. Out of respect I have changed the names of those involved although I am quite sure they would not mind their identities being revealed.

The Bird story

It was a warm August evening and everything was quiet as many were still on the beach enjoying the sunshine. A group of eighteen had gathered to listen to a lecture I was giving at the Integral Yoga Centre in Gibraltar. As I was speaking I saw a seagull come through the entrance of the Centre and start to walk towards us in the hall. I quietly conveyed to the audience what was happening, as they had their backs facing the entrance of the hall. "Don't panic. Stay calm. Look back slowly. There is a seagull walking straight up towards us!"

Everyone gently shifted to let the seagull through. Still in shock, we watched as the seagull walked towards me and jumped up on to the rostrum where I was seated. It stopped for a moment as if asking for permission, jumped onto the altar, bowed at the *Yantra* (a form of mandala) and then made its way back out of the hall towards the door and flew off! We were all dumbfounded and could not believe what we had seen. Seagulls are rather large and can be vicious. But this one seemed to know exactly what it wanted and where it wanted to go!

Some years later, I related this story during another lecture I was giving at the Gibraltar Yoga Centre. Some of the people in the audience were there on that fateful day and witnessed the seagull incident, so they were able to give credence to the story. They added that they all felt it was a sign of some sort from the Universe. After the lecture, Julie approached me and said, "Nalanie, I want a sign like that".

"Then ask the Universe for a sign!   Ask and you shall receive, seek and you shall find, knock and the door shall be open to you." I answered quoting from the New Testament.

I had been counselling Julie for over a year. She had tragically lost her daughter Sara because of a motorbike accident.   Sara left behind a toddler, a boy, whom Julie was looking after.   During the year I was counselling her she had started to have better days when she would laugh and actually allow herself to be happy. I told her Sara would want her to be a happy surrogate mom to her son.   She wouldn't want a miserable mother to bring up her child.   So Julie really tried but there were days she would feel guilty for being cheerful and she would ask how she could possibly be happy when she did not know if her daughter was happy, too. She wanted to know for sure and I would answer that none of us could be certain about such things, as we were still in a material world so we just need to trust and have faith.

A week after I told Julie to ask for a sign, she arrived late to the lecture I was giving and hurriedly placed her shoes just outside the hall.   The wearing of shoes was not permitted in the Yoga Hall for reasons of hygiene so we requested visitors to place their shoes in a special rack in the kitchen area of the Centre.   Often people would walk up to me at the end of the lecture to get a hug or to ask me something so I would frequently be occupied, but on this occasion I saw Julie leave the hall and then re-enter with something in her hands.   As she came closer, I noticed a little sparrow nestled in the palms of her hands and I asked her, "Julie, did you buy that cute little sparrow?"

Tears were rolling down her cheeks as she whispered, "No, Nalanie, I didn't buy this bird. You told me to ask for a sign so I asked God to give me sign in the form of a bird, to let me know Sara was happy, like what happened to all of you with the Seagull. I arrived late so I decided to leave my shoes right outside the hall. When I went out to retrieve my shoes, this little sparrow was lying inside one of them. I picked it up and brought it to show you. This is my sign! It is my Sara!"

I was as excited as she was and tears of joy formed in my eyes as I responded, "What will you do with the sparrow now?"

"I will take her outside and let her fly, and set her free."

A few of us walked with her to the entrance of the centre where she opened her palms and shouted, "Be happy Sara. Thank you for coming to let me know you are safe and happy. Stay free. I promise I will bring up my grandson with joy and tell him wonderful stories about his beautiful mother. Thank you for freeing me!"

Amazed and exuberant we watched as the sparrow flew away.

Cot Death

I first met Maggie when she attended one of my lectures at the Gibraltar Yoga Centre. A gentle yet flamboyant character she smiled constantly, but behind those eyes I sensed a deep sadness. One day she decided to take the Hatha Yoga basic teacher training course that I was offering at the centre. I always stipulate for all such courses that every participant has a good knowledge of Raja Yoga, the spiritual aspect and real meaning of Yoga. Yoga is too often considered to be only about physical exercise (Hatha Yoga), the postures to help with flexibility and strength, and the true spiritual meaning of it is frequently overlooked. I have noticed throughout my career that Hatha Yoga students who are not well versed with the real teachings of Yoga can totally misunderstand the depth of the teaching of Hatha.

A few months into the course Maggie asked if she could see me privately, which I affirmed and the following week she came to the centre for a consultation.

"I lost my baby fifteen years ago through cot death. I have been to therapy and I thought I was getting better, but during this course a lot of issues have come up. After a lot of introspection, I have come to realise that I still feel a lot of anger. I constantly shout at my husband but I now recognize that it's not him I am annoyed at. I am furious that my husband and I were sleeping while our baby died. She was only six weeks old. How could I not know? I am still carrying the guilt and I am blaming everybody else for it. Over the years I have served at charity events for the benefit of sick or underprivileged children and I assumed that it would release this guilt that I feel all the time. But it hasn't. I just can't seem to shake off this emotion no matter how hard I try."

"Maggie, how can it be your fault when you loved her so much? Things happen to all of us. Some good, some bad, some terrible. It's just life. You can recall the circumstances of the death over and over and wish as much as you like that things were different. But no matter how many times these thoughts rotate in your mind, you are never ever going to be able to change the past. So, first thing we will do is to release the guilt by forgiving yourself of a fault that was never yours in the first place. I will teach you a visualization specifically for that, and which you must perform a few times every day. Next, we are going to perform a little puja ceremony for that beautiful child and we are going to let her go. Your sorrow keeps her entrapped between worlds. You need to set both of you free. It's time to cut the umbilical cord. Are you ready for that? Remember, energy never dies, it transforms into something else. None of us die, we just change costumes." I then showed her the quote from *The Living Gita** that I often use to reassure people:

'Whoever truly knows the Self, indestructible, eternal, birthless and changeless, in what way would such a person kill? Who would be killed? Just like casting off worn out clothing and putting on new ones, that which is embodied casts out worn out bodies and enters others that are new.

Weapons do not affect the Self, water does not wet it, and wind does not dry it, fire does not burn it.

The Self cannot be pierced or cut; it cannot be burned, moistened or dried. It is endless, all pervading, stable and immovable and everlasting. Knowing all this, there is no cause to grieve.'

(Living Gita Chapter 2, Slokas 21 to 25)

Maggie did the visualizations. We performed the ceremony during which she voiced everything she wanted to say to her departed daughter. After the ceremony she looked at me and said, "She was here, my angel was here!"

And then Maggie cried, and she laughed as I had never heard her laugh before. She went home and apologized to her husband for all the years of blame and anger. Now they were all free.

The Living Gita is a translation of the sacred Hindu text, *The Bhagavad Gita*
by Sri Swami Satchidananda

Besides deepening the work with my clients, I was finding much joy being in the presence of my children and grandchildren. Tara and Tasha spent many weekends with me, which provided the respite I needed from the pain. We would watch Disney movies, dance, laugh, sing and play games! Every Monday for the first two years after Shanky's passing, when I was not travelling, we would organize a babysitter and Shani, Andrew and myself would go out for dinner and just relish our time together. They needed healing, too. We were such a close family and Shanky left a huge void in all our lives.

The following year we travelled to Singapore where Shaman, Hersha and Indira met up with us for a short family holiday. Indira, dear Indy as we called her, is like a character from a Disney movie. Her charm, intelligence and joy are infectious for one so little. I felt it was so important to keep this bond alive. I had seen death tear so many families apart. The inability to deal with sorrow would generate anger, which turned into bitterness and self-pity. It never made sense to me, as it only caused more pain. I did not want to ignore my duty as a mother. We loved being together and spoke of Shanky all the time as if he was still physically with us. I felt Shaman was still deeply in sorrow, although he did a great job of hiding it. I spoke quietly to him and asked him if he had cried, and he answered that he could not. His father's death threw him off balance and he found it hard to come to terms with what life was all about.

"Mom, I don't understand the point of life, if in the end we all die! Nothing makes sense. Why bother?"

"Shaman, all I know is that the point of life is right here, right now in front of me. I see you and your loving relationship with your family, with Hersha and Indy. The point for me is that it is all about love. We are here for a short time and for some reason when we feel love and share it, it fills our hearts and our souls! And these rays of love penetrate those around us. Your dad loved you, loved us all, and his life was devoted to giving us his best. This is the legacy we must pass on. Look at your sister, Shani, and with all her hardship she inspires us with her love for the girls and the selfless love she pours on Talia. Watching her fills our hearts with admiration. This love is the purpose of life."

Love, that wonderful deep healing love I always knew was there but had become masked by the pain I felt, once more started to filter into every aspect of my life. Family, friends, work, teaching, serving the community – it all made me feel so rich and abundant! There are days that I feel my heart will burst with the love I feel! Yes, I had found my Lord of Love and the miracles started to roll in daily. Simple miracles. Signs everywhere. My life and my connection with the Divine Consciousness had grown beyond my comprehension. My world had become a magical place. There was not one day, and there still isn't even after 12 years, that I don't think of Shanky. Sometimes I experience a sharp pain but most of the time now I think of him and love wells up in my heart accompanied only by a gentle ache.

But I didn't know that this evolution of my personality was opening me up for something very special to happen in my life.

Some of the principal characters in the movie called 'my life'

Our last weekend away together:
With my late husband, Shanky Chellaram,

Our last Christmas together:
(L to R) Me, Talia, Andrew,
Natasha, Tara, Shani and
Shanky

Our last Christmas:
Shanky with Hersha,
Shaman, Natasha
and Tara

*The surprise gift:
In Marrakesh with
Marina*

*Les and I with members of the
Gibraltar Sangha: Julio is
second on the left standing.
His beloved Paddy is kneeling
far left, and Shanti and Lilian
'Lakshmi' are at the front*

*With my siblings: Back row: Me, Kumar and Maj
Front row: David, Lavi, Mira and Kantu*

"Truth is one, paths are many"
H H Sri Swami Satchidananda
Founder of Integral Yoga and
my beloved Gurudev

At the feet of my Master:
With Gurudev during his
visit to Gibraltar in 1997

My first Gurus: My Dad
George Harilela with my
Mom, Chandra

Back to work: Giving a talk in Hong Kong organised by my sister Mira.

Back to work: Speaking at a Peace Festival by the Brandenburg Gate in Berlin in 2009 with Lakshmi and Paddy Alcantara (far left)

*Back to work: Outside an eye hospital in India in 2010
(L to R) Krssy, Paddy Crouch, Chandra, Janaki, Les
Mr Ramaswamy, myself, the Head of the hospital, Swami Lalitananda
Shanti and Lucy 'Luckshmi' and two of the hospital staff.*

Happy again!
Our blessing
with Mataji

Happy again! I learned that I could
love Les and still keep Shanky in my
heart

The family all together (Back row L to R) Shaman, Hersha,
Me, Les, Natasha, Shani, Andrew, Tara
(Front row L to R) Indy, Shahan and Talia

Loss, Life, Love

Book Three

Love

Chapter 1
Falling In Love Again

Wise men say only fools rush in,
But I can't help falling in love with you.
Shall I stay?
Would it be a sin
If I can't help falling in love with you?
Like a river flows surely to the sea
Darling so it goes
Some things are meant to be.

(From the song "Can't Help Falling in Love" written by
Hugo Peretti, Luigi Creatore & George David Weiss)

In the spring of 2010, Les and I were developing a deep friendship. We were working closely together on our charities, both of us driven by our goals to make a better world for those we touch. And both of us touched by death. We realized that if we were going to be alive then the Divine had kept us here for a purpose. A purpose greater than ourselves. What that was we were eager to discover.

His separation from his wife two years prior and his narrow escape from cancer spiralled his soul journey. His love for a 'God' without distinction and his passionate search for the truth were inspirational. Over the course of the year he had turned vegetarian, he was initiated and asked me to provide him with a Sanskrit name. Initiation is where a teacher endowed with blessings from an authentic Guru passes a mantra onto the initiate. His Sanskrit name is *Anand*, meaning 'bliss'. He had adopted Swami Satchidananda as his Guru, and me as a personal friend and a guide on his journey of spiritual awakening. He was popular with the *sangha* members as his demeanour was always gentle, kind and highly motivated. Whenever we needed help at the Yoga centre for whatever jobs, he was always there. His open mindedness and willingness to examine different opinions with great humility was one of the traits I loved about him. And primarily, his support for women's rights and equality for all mankind made him even more attractive in my eyes.

Les is a year older than I am so we grew up in the same era but our backgrounds couldn't be more different. You could say we were poles apart. I was born into a wealthy Hindu family and grew up in Hong Kong where I attended a Catholic School. Later I attended Pepperdine University in the US immediately following which, I got married and moved to Gibraltar. Les was born into a working class family in England, in a town on the border with Wales and his heritage was predominantly Welsh. His mother was a devout Christian and Les underwent a strict Baptist upbringing, which according to him raised more questions about God than it could answer. He left school at the age of sixteen and got a job so he could help support his family, as his father was out of work due to illness. Three years later he went back to education, attending college to catch up on qualifications he had missed out on. He married young (around the same time I got married) had two children and began a career literally starting at the bottom, as a clerk in an office. In 1978 he began a course of home study and, through hard work and total dedication, within 5 years had climbed to the pinnacle of his career. But his meteoric rise came at a price and in 1983 he suffered a nervous breakdown caused by overwork. Everything fell apart at that point. He couldn't bring himself to reveal to anyone how he was feeling and hid his condition as best he could, thinking it was a sign of weakness. He openly admits it was the biggest mistake of his life because his stubbornness to accept he needed help cost him his job, his home and everything in it when his wife filed for divorce. He walked away with just two suitcases yet his greatest regret was the pain the separation caused his two young children, Francesca and Gregg.

Believing that 'change is as good as a rest' Les moved to London where, despite his condition, he managed to find employment. He also met a young Gibraltarian woman and in 1989 they moved to Gibraltar to start a new life together. They married in 1991 but it was a difficult relationship and destined not to last. Their interests were too dissimilar and they had separate goals in life, and despite having two children together, Bradley and Sian, they eventually drifted apart. He later admitted that, when he met his second wife he was on the rebound from his first marriage. At the time, despite agreeing to the divorce he was still in love with his first wife but he accepted full responsibility for the breakup and decided to let her go.

So Les had two failed marriages behind him and came with a lot of baggage all of which were the main cause of my reticence to become involved with him. And yet, despite this and our vastly differing backgrounds we had so much else in common. In fact, it was uncanny just how much synchronicity we had.

Fine Arts were my major at University and as a student I loved spending hours in museums, enjoyed ballet and classical music. Shanky never really enjoyed any of those things. He loved anything to do with computers; anything to do with trading on markets; he enjoyed going to the Theatre at the West End of London and his favourite pastime was eating out. Whenever we were in London, he would take me to some marvellous shows and great restaurants. Our holidays were always very short, as we had limited time. Our itinerary was quite full with purchasing goods for the shops in Gibraltar and spending time with our children who were in boarding school. We always had to rush back to Gibraltar to manage the shops so museums were out of the question. They were the last things on Shanky's list. I recall one holiday when I requested that we visit the British Museum and he actually agreed. When we arrived there he said, "I will wait for you outside. See you in 10 minutes."

"What? Ten minutes? I will have hardly any time to go around one room!"

"Well," he said, "then fifteen minutes otherwise we won't have time to do other things."

I rushed around like a lunatic and hardly saw anything. I think back now and I laugh at myself! What an idiot I was! I should have told him to return to the hotel or browse around his favourite shops because I wanted to take my time and I did not care if I missed going shopping. But back then I believed it was selfish of me to express my wants so instead I started seething inside. I remember that evening as if it were yesterday. I was angry and blamed him for being selfish when it had nothing to do with him. He was saying his truth. It was my weakness and warped sense of being gracious that caused all the confusion. I learnt later that *'goodness is not weakness'* - and vice versa - and being assertive was a positive action, whereas being aggressive only caused misunderstandings and unnecessary grief.

As my meditation practices developed together with the study of spiritual books, I felt myself transforming from a narrow, personal viewpoint to a larger and more compassionate understanding of my emotions. If only they taught such things in schools! The world would be a happier place. My beloved master passed on this gem of wisdom to all his students:

A perfect action is one that causes no harm to anyone, some benefit to someone, yourself included.

This powerful statement altered the course of my life. I became more courageous, felt more empowered and less insecure.

Les, an artist himself, loved museums, classical music and operas and when he discovered that I shared these same interests, he was eager to share his knowledge with me. I had so much to absorb from these arts that had been ignored for years. We spent many evenings listening to Rachmaninoff, operas, mantras and all kinds of music. *'If music be the food of love, play on'* as William Shakespeare said so beautifully! And we found ourselves falling in love with each other. This was daunting for me but at the same time exhilarating and I looked forward to our meetings. We charged each wonderful moment with laughter, and felt impish just spending time doing things we both loved. We realized we had so many similarities. Les said his ex-wife, like Shanky, hadn't appreciated classical music and fine arts so both of us seemed to have cast aside many of our hobbies to please our partners.

I felt as if I was sixteen again and so did he. At first I was embarrassed by this emotion, after all, I was fifty-six years old and a grandmother! How could this happen? I was still grieving over Shanky. How was it possible to fall for someone else? So I called my eldest sister Mira and told her of my feelings. Instead of being upset with me, she was delighted that I had met someone.

"Sis, I am so happy for you. It is possible to love two people at the same time. Shanky is no longer in the body and he was worried about you living on your own. Didn't he write the song that said he wished you would meet someone else?"

"Yes, he did." And the lyrics of the last stanza of his song came back to me:

> *'I wish you happiness and hope one day you'll find.*
> *Another one to take my place and bring you peace of mind.*
> *Till then I'll stay with you. I'll always be right here.*
> *You only have to call my name and your pain will disappear.'*

The next thing I did was to tell my children Shani and Shaman. I wanted them to be the first to know that I was dating Les. I told them it was very early days in the relationship and I had no answers. I just knew that we both were enjoying each other's company and we laughed a lot together. I must admit internally it was hard for me, as deep inside I was concerned they would be annoyed at their bohemian mom. Like a true Yogi, though, I faced my fear and told them anyway!

Shani was pleased for me. I felt she carried the guilt that, because she was so busy with her three girls and her business, she couldn't do what she wanted for me. Now, she could relax knowing someone was there to take me out and have some fun. All my married life I had been looking after children, the shop, the dance school and the Yogis, and I realized I rarely had time to do the things I loved besides meditation. That was and is my greatest love. To connect with God and remind myself that I am spirit having a worldly experience is one thing I never sacrificed. Every day for over thirty years I have spent time in meditation. It was and is my medicine, my raison d'etre. A great reminder that I am energy.

Shani had met Les and really liked him. He had the highest regard for her and the selfless and dedicated way she looked after Talia. He constantly reiterated at the beginning of our relationship that somebody should document Talia's progress as a consequence of Shani's unselfish love and pure perseverance. He insisted that what Shani was doing and had achieved was so inspirational it had to be put on film. Four years later, it was he (together with his friend Danny Bugeja under their video production label *Alta Vida Productions*) who filmed and directed *"Energy For Life: Talia's Story"*, a 50 minute documentary that was premiered at Leisure Cinemas in Gibraltar following which it was broadcast by the Gibraltar TV channel 'GBC' and released on YouTube. The story was told. Love heals; it is the energy for life. It took him three years of hard work. I was so touched that he executed this huge project with unperturbed dedication.

Shaman, on the other hand, was a bit dubious. He wondered whether I was falling for Les just because I was replacing Shanky. I reassured him that I wasn't because, as characters, they were as different as chalk and cheese. In time, as he got to know Les better, he grew to love him too. As for my grandchildren, they enjoyed his company and spent much time with both of us. Tara only asked one thing of me and that was, 'Gran, never marry him!'

Some of the *sangha* members were extremely shocked by my actions, and some even left the Centre. They felt that after Shanky had passed I should have become a monk and dedicated the rest of my life to selfless service. Falling in love with another man simply didn't fit their impression of me sitting high on the pedestal they had mentally placed me upon!

This was very interesting for me to observe and taught me a lot about both myself and about others. I had a huge battle inside of me for at least the first three years Les and I were together. The truth was that I was contented on my own. I only wanted to serve God and humanity. Where did I have time to devote myself to another human being? I was free to do whatever I liked. But then, I felt free with Les. We had great times and loved being with each other. This dichotomy left me feeling uncomfortable and indecisive. My mind had been so clear and now it became fuzzy. Was the affair with him worth it? Should I drop it? How could I disturb the minds of *sangha* members or the community at large? Was that selfish? Simultaneously, I felt strong and stuck to my convictions. Always a rebel, I realised I could not depend on anyone else's opinion. I had to find out for myself. Loving Les did not diminish my love for others but served to strengthen it. I felt I was bubbling over with love and wanting to share more with the world. How could that be wrong? The ego and the Self were having a field day in the realm of my mind stuff yet amidst all that noisy thinking, I felt extremely calm and witnessed the play of life. I found it more than just interesting; it was fascinating! I was exploring the whole framework of human emotions and the subject was myself, and this time around from a different perspective.

Coming from a Hindu background, I was expected to mourn my husband for the rest of my life. It was hard for many in my tradition to see me with Les. I comprehended their dilemma; it was their indoctrination and belief system. My siblings were all marvellous, and when they met him for the first time during my brother Maj's 60th birthday party in Bangkok they showered him with kindness and acceptance, even though some of them were shocked by my actions. I was ecstatic! It was a huge step for me to introduce him to my family and I was so grateful to them for their graciousness. We were all just so happy to be with each other. I am really not a 'party person' but Maj's 60th birthday party was so special. After Shanky's death I appreciated how short and fragile life can be so I began to value everyone so much more, and I became determined to spend more time with my siblings in the future.

Most of my clients who had lost a spouse or partner and came to me for consultations had similar emotions. Fear and guilt dominated their minds, and they felt they no longer had the right to be happy. When they witnessed my life restarting, it gave them hope and many were able to cut loose from their negative emotions and archaic judgments. We are social creatures that have often been made to feel guilty by senseless conventions and misunderstood religious dogma!

For generation upon generation much of the populace has been taught that we do not have the right to be happy, which is the antithesis of spirituality! Where did it come from? The concept of original sin? How is it that we have grown to believe we are born sinners? Some religions teach that unless we suffer we cannot know God. In reality, many do come to the spiritual path through suffering because there are no answers to be found in the realm of physicality. But that does not infer that we *have* to suffer to find God. Ultimately, relief from suffering can only be found in the sphere of Consciousness. Once we truly understand that we are spirit then attachment to things on the material spectrum starts to fade. The realization that nothing is ours and that everything is on loan, including ourselves, opens the door to the search for something more permanent. The theory of sacrifice and suffering has been misinterpreted and miscommunicated for years and has left a structure so contradictory to its veracity.

I recall a time when Gurudeva visited Spain and Shanky and I took him to visit a cathedral in the town of Ronda. Whilst inside, he abruptly jumped into the confessional box (thank goodness there were no priests around!) and called to me through the little grille on the side of the box.

"Nalanie, come here, right now."

As I approached the confessional box, I remember thinking, *'what have I done wrong? Did I say something nonsensical?'*

His voice boomed out. "How dare you call yourself a sinner! You are a child of God!"

For a moment I was stunned by this proclamation! It was as if he had blasted something so huge out of my psyche that I almost fell to the ground from the power of it. That evening, whilst contemplating this episode, it came to me that for years I believed I was never good enough, and in a flash my Master had washed it all away. *I was a child of God and, as such, I was loved without condition.*

This is what we call the *shakti* (energy) of the Guru. He or she has the power to show us the truth in an instant. It is the awakening of this massive force that gave me the courage to follow my heart throughout all my dilemmas.

I also realised that so long as we are alive, we will always be tested. And the more resilient one became, the harder the tests. The road to the Light of the Spirit is lined with thorns alongside the roses.

The transition we make is we no longer see suffering as a punishment but rather a device that pushes us forwards and upwards on our spiritual journey.

It seemed that in my life, on my spiritual journey, I first had to experience material and physical losses. As I became accustomed to them, I then endured the path of surrendering those desires and emotions that were no longer required for my growth and only served to slow or stall the journey. With Shanky's death, I had to traverse a passage of fire in order to continue to the Light of the Spirit. Life, I have understood, is the quest to be free from all that keeps us imprisoned in darkness. I honestly learnt that truly nothing was mine. The Light showed me how temporary everything was, so my decision was either to embrace everything with a passion and love so profound, or else to deny it all and retreat to a cave where I could just exist in peace. I scrutinized my personality and noted that with the one I had been given (or was it the one I had created for myself?) there was only one choice: to love the world of differences and learn to transcend the dualities by developing my spiritual muscles. And how was I to do that? By accepting pain as a purifying process and then by using that knowledge to help others who get caught in the wheel of suffering. Armed with this understanding, I forged onwards with my relationship with Les. Let me embrace whatever life presents and yes, I deserve to be happy!

Alas, the terrain was not smooth, instead quite arduous. The first few months of a new relationship always seem like a breeze. Yet adjusting and adapting to different ways and habits are not that simple. We had to break up three times before we both found that balance. Each time we separated fate twisted the course of events till finally we had to surrender to its will!

But I have jumped ahead. The year was coming to a close and I had decided to travel to India to donate the money we had raised through my talks and fundraising events to a few different projects over there. Whenever I travelled, I invited those who wanted to experience the joy of service overseas together with the adventure and knowledge it brings. So for the trip to India I was joined by my P.A. Shanti, Cynthia 'Chandra' Walker, Lucy 'Luckshmi' Cannon, my niece Krssy Harilela, Jennie 'Janaki' Macdonald and her partner Paddy Crouch. Les also decided to travel with us, as it was his dream to visit India and the children his charity was sponsoring there. Luckshmi and I organized the itinerary and everyone was excited to go. What we didn't realize at that time was how much of an adventure it would turn out to be.

About a month prior to leaving for India, I asked Andrew to look for a property for me. One night I received a message in a dream telling me it was time to move. The dream confirmed what I was beginning to accept. During the course of the year I had received many visitors and my small apartment was now impractical. In addition, my grandchildren could no longer fit in one bed with me, as they were growing up. If I was to continue to entertain visitors - to me 'guest is God', a chance to serve - then I needed something bigger. Property prices had tumbled considerably and I sensed it was a good time to buy. I heard my father's voice in the back of my mind when I told him I was going to sell the penthouse in Gibraltar so that Shanky and I could move to Spain. He agreed so long as I promised I would buy a home that I loved when the opportunity presented itself. And I promised him I would. Shanky and I had rented an apartment and I now felt it was time to fulfil that pledge. We looked at a few properties and eventually found a beautiful 3-bedroom apartment that I could easily afford. The price had fallen to almost half its original value so I told Andrew I would take it because it was such a good deal. He turned around and said to me, "Nalanie, before you make the final decision, I have seen a house in Sotogrande that I believe you will like. And there is potential there to build a Yoga centre."

Since moving to Spain I had given *satsangs* in all sorts of places; from one student's home to another, and in the conference rooms at hotels and spa clubs. Anywhere that could fit my customarily modest yet enthusiastic audiences. It would be fantastic to have a dedicated place in Spain where we could hold regular *satsangs*, Yoga courses and other events to promote and develop spiritual growth, and where we could form another *sangha*. But did I really want the responsibility of looking after a larger home? Did I really need that with all the travelling I undertook every year to teach Yoga courses, give spiritual talks and do charity work?

Intrigued, I replied, "OK Andrew, I will look but I doubt if I would be interested, and I am not sure if I can afford to buy in that area. I do love looking at properties, though, so let's go check it out!"

Sotogrande is an exclusive area of large villas and expensive apartments, golf courses and polo fields, and surrounded by beautiful trees and landscaped gardens. It is the 'Beverly Hills' of the Costa del Sol where many rich and famous people live or have second homes, and I was not sure I wanted to be living amongst such opulence especially as I only had my inheritance to live on. I wasn't charging for teaching and I was concerned what money I had would dwindle away.

As we approached the house, the owners, a sweet, elderly retired couple greeted us at the door. I immediately took to them and noticed that the wife was shaking. *'Parkinson's'*, I thought. The gentleman later told me that it was indeed Parkinson's disease and that was why they were selling their home. They wanted to return to the UK where his wife would receive the best medical attention that she needed. As he showed us around his home, I could feel his sadness. I told him I was a Yoga therapist and I offered to talk to his wife if he approved. He did and, leaving Andrew to take the measurements he needed to put the property on the general market, we had a short but lovely therapy session.

The house was very small, no more than a two-bedroom bungalow, and in dire need of redecoration. However, there was a huge terrace on which a Jacuzzi had been placed and a barbecue area had been built complete with bricked benches and a chimney. The garden was exquisite, well tended and bordered by a tall hedge, which ensured privacy. There was something magical about that garden.

Then something strange happened. I envisioned a Yoga hall with large glass doors built on top of the extensive terrace, and I saw myself living in that home! My brain was already ticking away, thinking of ways to raise enough money to build the Yoga hall my mind had conjured up. My imagination was running wild and yet there were doubts. The money I had would never stretch that far so maybe I should just say, 'no'. When would I have time to sort out renovations and organize building works? I was about to leave for India! No, my dream was to simplify my life, not to give myself more to do. Then I heard a voice speaking to me saying, *'Nalanie do not make a decision yet. Trust in the highest order.'*

When we got back into Andrew's car to drive home, he asked me what I thought.

"Andrew, the house has great potential. And yes, you are right, I could build a Yoga hall on the terrace. But I do not have enough funds to buy the house and to do it up, let alone contemplate building the hall. I know they have brought the price down significantly, but I couldn't afford it unless they come down by a further hundred thousand Euros. Only then can I consider buying it, and I can use the hundred thousand to renovate it. But nobody will bring the price down that much. Please tell them the truth and tell them I don't mean to insult their integrity. I know I have to make a decision this week to take either the house or the apartment, which would really be my choice. I will be off to India in two weeks and then after that to Hong Kong to visit the family* so I would be really grateful if they can come back to me quickly either accepting or rejecting my offer."

Andrew replied, "I'll make the offer to them tonight. I doubt that they will agree but we will try anyway."

That evening before going to bed I prayed for guidance, as I always do whenever I have to make a big decision.

"Dearest Beloved Divine source, if I am meant to serve in this house; if it is for the greater good; then allow the price to be reduced by one hundred thousand Euros. If it is not meant to be, know that I will be equally happy, if not happier, in the apartment. Thy will be done."

I went to sleep absolutely convinced that the owners of the home would not agree. I felt bad. I honestly did not want to offend them by making such a low offer. But I also knew I had to listen to that inner voice and I had to trust it.   The following morning, I got up as usual with no expectations, and then my phone rang. It was Andrew.

*In June 2010, Hersha had given birth to a beautiful boy. She and Shaman named him Shahan and I travelled to Hong Kong to officiate his blessing. Now I was longing to see Indira and Shahan again.

"Nalanie, they have agreed."

"What? Are you sure? I don't believe it!"

"Yes. Me too, I am quite stunned that they agreed! What do you want me to do now?"

"Andrew, I made a deal with God last night. I said if I am meant to serve, my offer would be accepted. If not, I would take the apartment. The choice has been made for me. Tell them I will go ahead. Ask them how much deposit they need and I will organize payment immediately."

"Are you sure about this? It's a massive undertaking and there's a lot of renovations you need to consider."

"Yes, I'm sure," I replied, not without some trepidation! "Can you give me the name of a good construction company and help me to make an appointment with them to see the home as soon as possible? With the reduction in the price, I have the funds to start work as soon as the deal is done."

After that, as with many things in my life, everything just flowed. I met up with the builders and we agreed the price. I told them the limit I had to spend and what I wanted done. I also asked them to quote what it would cost to build a large hall on the terrace adjacent to the home. Within ten days, they had drawn up simple plans for me to consent to before I left for India. While I was away, they would start the ball rolling by applying for the requisite building permits and licences, and other formalities.

Then they quoted the cost of building the Yoga hall. They estimated it would cost around ninety thousand Euros. I told them it was impossible for the moment. My thinking cap was on and I was already visualizing giving *satsangs* and courses to raise funds to build the hall brick by brick. I was both ecstatic and terrified at the prospect. The typical state of a human mind in such circumstances but, again, I was grateful that I could shut off the fearful negative voice in my head and listen to the positive one. Was I taking a risk gambling away my livelihood? Then again, I reasoned if I don't take any risks life would never move forward. I pacified myself by repeating the absolute truth, which was that I was actually purchasing land! One thousand square metres of it in a beautiful area. If anything did go wrong, I would just sell it.

I turned my mind towards India. Excited at the direction my life was taking I got ready for the trip and left the rest of the formalities surrounding the house to Andrew. He was more than capable of handling such matters for me while I was away. Prior to departing I asked Les to come with me to see the house. He loved it but at the same time he did not seem happy for me. I was surprised at his behaviour. I thought he would be as excited as I was. His melancholy demeanour made me doubt our relationship and I was beginning to feel uncomfortable in his presence. And, of course, I told him how I was feeling. With everything going on with the property and the preparation for the trip I had no choice but to tell him my doubts and fears whilst we were on the flight to India. He was naturally hurt and upset at my words, and couldn't understand them no matter how much I tried to explain that I cared for him but I just couldn't deal with so much negativity when life was finally beginning to make sense to me again after Shanky's passing. I apologized and said I just felt that maybe we were not meant to be together. By the time we landed in India his mood was sullen whereas mine was full of enthusiasm for the work we were about to embark on and the people we were to meet. I felt sorry that he reacted the way he did. I *expected* - there goes that word that always causes problems - yes, I expected him to be more understanding and apologize to me for being upset when I bought the house. But that did not happen. Instead he thought me selfish to speak about such things and spoil his trip to India. As Gurudeva always told us, *'don't make an appointment or you will be dis-appointed.'*

There are two sides to every story and I realize our palettes were truly quite different, which is fine when one is young but at my age, I was not ready to change my palette to please anyone.

I often make this statement whenever people try to goad me into a situation that I do not want. I respond that I have only one boss and that is my God and its name is *peace*. Falling in love with the world again seemed so much easier than falling in love with one person.

"Wise men say only fools rush in...."

Chapter 2
India

We arrived in Chennai where we met Swami Divyananda (an Integral Yoga monk initiated by Gurudeva) and a disciple of his by the name of Senthil. I had heard Senthil was a fantastic soul whose family looked after the ashram that Gurudeva once managed in Sri Lanka and that was now lying empty and dilapidated. That evening over dinner Senthil and I discussed working together to revive it, and I told him about our plans and what we were going to do whilst in India.

I related to Senthil that for several years the Integral Yoga centre in Gibraltar had been supporting an amazing man called Papa Vidyaakar, and one of the main objectives of this trip to India was to see first hand the work he was doing. His story was remarkable and his cause was truly a noble and inspirational one, and we could not miss the opportunity of meeting with this humble and incredible human being.

Many years ago, seeing such poverty and misery around him, Papa Vidyaakar was moved to try to do something about it. He began by rescuing homeless children, taking them off the streets and housing them in a small makeshift orphanage. In the 10 years the Yoga Centre had supported him he was able to progress from one single room facility to several purpose built centres, called *Udavam Karangal*, situated all over India. In addition, as his reputation grew and more and more sponsors and supporters came to his aid, he was able to establish refuge centres for women and children with physical handicaps and mental health problems. During our trip to India we had arranged to visit a new facility he had set up close to Chennai.

I then informed Senthil of our plans to visit two eye hospitals based in Coimbatore that had been introduced to us by a good friend of Integral Yoga, Mr Ramaswamy who was the Chairperson of the India-based *Roots Corporation*. The Integral Yoga centre in Gibraltar had collected enough funds to pay for three hundred eye operations for the villagers in the surrounding area who could not afford the treatment, which was mainly to remove cataracts.

After Coimbatore we were to visit an orphanage in Mysore where my niece Tiana was taking time off to study the Yogic Sciences. She suggested the Integral Yoga centre support the orphanage and, of course, we readily agreed.

From there our hectic schedule would take us to Andhra Pradesh to meet a Catholic priest by the name of Father Mabu. A few years earlier Les's charity, AKIN, had been approached by the Catholic Church in Gibraltar to support Father Mabu who, it was claimed, was struggling to help the orphans and poor families in his parish. So Les took it upon faith and duly began sending small regular amounts to the impoverished priest. As Father Mabu was in effect a referral by the Catholic Church this was the first - and only - project undertaken by AKIN without prior vetting to ensure the legitimacy of the request for financial support. Les had never met Father Mabu so the purpose of this visit was to get to know him and the work he was doing.

Finally, after Andhra Pradesh we were to return to Chennai and then fly home.

All the team were laughing and participating in the conversation with Senthil except for Les who was sitting quietly and not saying much. Because of his temperament I decided not to introduce him as someone I had been dating but rather as a member of our *sangha*. I must say I was quite embarrassed by his moodiness and was grateful that I got to see that part of his nature before getting too serious with him.

The team then retreated to bed early and the following morning we headed off to see Papa Vidyaakar. When we arrived at his *Udavam Karangal* Centre we couldn't believe our eyes! It was beautiful, set in well-tended and colourful gardens and surrounded by a tall brick wall it exuded a peaceful and loving atmosphere. It really was a safe haven for those who lived there and desperately needed it.

Papa Vidyaakar came out to greet us and I was so overwhelmed to be in his presence I felt compelled to bow at his feet. Such was his humility I think this token of respect and admiration made him feel a little uncomfortable and he quickly bade me to stand up.

What a man! What service! There were over two thousand homeless people residing at his sanctuary, which was divided into four separate buildings around a quadrant. One section was both an orphanage and a school where the orphans were provided with clean living conditions and classrooms equipped to provide them with primary education. The next section was the main dining hall, which provided meals for all at the refuge; the third section housed the mentally affected and the last was an edifice built for those who were physically disabled. Medical staff and psychologists were working round the clock thanks to donations provided by the many organizations that had been moved by his altruism.

The team chatted with many of the women and children living there, and as we held the little ones who ran up to us to receive hugs our hearts were bursting with love. Fulfilled but exhausted we made our way back to the hotel and retired early.

Service is the road to freedom. When one sees so much suffering, one's own suffering fades into insignificance.

The next day we flew to Coimbatore. We stayed at the Integral Yoga ashram where Mr Ramaswamy had arranged for us to be treated like royalty. For the staff at the ashram, Balu the manager, Dr. Thilikavathy and Kartekeyan, nothing was too much trouble. They organized sightseeing tours for us, to the different temples that our Master stayed in whilst searching for his path to God.

These were precious moments when we revelled in the deep spirit that is India. The colours, the prayers, the people, the crowds, the poverty, the exuberance, all blended in a potpourri of enchanted moments. The holy places adorned with beautiful flowers and sweet scents that entice the soul and yet, there was also the subtle calling from priests whispering 'money, money, money'. At times it wasn't subtle, nor did they whisper! I wondered if they were truly interested in saving our souls or captivated by what they could get out of us. This is the dichotomy that is India and we couldn't help falling in love with it. India showed us the best of the human spirit and the worst of it. Therein lies the real pilgrimage. The outside world introduces us to our inner world. We are constantly presented with extreme opposites. Which do we choose, that which tickles the ego or brings us to the higher Self?

India reflected my inner thoughts. I looked at Les and felt his anger towards me. I was sorry I had spoilt his trip. I was hoping he would step up and be stronger but instead he withdrew into this person that I hardly knew with drooping shoulders, and frowning constantly. Yet I knew he was such a kind and gentle soul. My words had deeply affected him.

India introduced me to a new domain of emotions that I thought I had left behind. Now it was up to me to decide which path I was to take. I was curious to see how the pilgrimage into my emotions would turn out.

From there we ventured to Mysore where we met Kanchana, a strong, determined woman who had established a small *Montessori* school for children. Alongside the school was a room that acted as a small 'cottage industry' facility where the mothers could work to earn some money while their children attended school. There they made many items such as wallets, slippers, ties and other products from recycled and leftover materials. Many of these women lived with husbands who were abusive or alcoholics. By teaching them a trade, Kanchana was opening the door to a better future for them. If they became financially independent, they would be able to fend for themselves and their children. We all enjoyed being with Kanchana, I admired her no-nonsense attitude and her straightforwardness, and we bought some of the items the mothers had made.

Kanchana was able to break away from her duties temporarily and join us on our journey to our next destination, which was half an hour from where the school was situated. There we met with Tiana, my niece, and she took us to the orphanage that she and the other Yoga students were supporting. It was a small, simple place and the children entertained us singing mantras led by one of the Yoga students who was a part time volunteer teacher there. We all joined in and sang along with them. Oh, to see those lovely dark eyes and those beautiful smiles really uplifted my spirit! I wanted to just hug them all and take them home with me! Then we were abruptly called out of our reverie by the owner of the orphanage who had arrived to meet us and to collect the money we had raised for the children. One look at him and my heart sank! My instincts screamed out at me, '*Nalanie, do NOT trust this man'.* He was overweight, unshaven and chewing *paan* (or *gutka,* a form of chewing tobacco commonly used in India) and displayed a disgusting array of yellow and black teeth when he smiled. We chatted for a while and he kept asking for the money we had brought. Suddenly, I had a brainwave!

"Yes," I said, "we have brought the money, and my niece Tiana mentioned to me that some of the children need to visit the dentist, and they need shoes and a few other things. I know how busy you are looking after these children so I have asked her to keep the money and make sure the children get what they need. Don't you think this is a brilliant idea? That way there is no extra work for you and the Yogis can perform karma yoga by overseeing the dental appointments and shopping for the shoes."

I must say I enjoyed the stunned look on his face.

"No, no, no, it is no trouble for us to take these children to the dentist," he said.

"You are so kind", I replied, determined not to hand the money directly to him. "But I cannot deny Tiana and her friends the chance to do good service."

I actually felt sorry for him. He got up in a huff and left! Kanchana looked at me and grinned. On our way out, she whispered, "you did the right thing."

The last part of our journey proved the most electrifying of adventures. Leaving Mysore we had no clue about what lay ahead in Andhra Pradesh.

We arrived at Vijayawada airport where Father Mabu had arranged to greet us. A minibus and a driver had been organised for the time we were there, but Father Mabu had arrived separately in a sparkling white *Ambassador,* a car he later claimed belonged to his bishop. The first impression I had on seeing him was *something is terribly wrong.* He was wearing a pure white shirt ironed and starched as if it had just come out from a Laundromat. His plump countenance conveyed his love for food, and there were two men with him who were wearing gold chains and looking every inch like bodyguards. How could one look so impeccable when working with impoverished families and orphans in the roughest and dirtiest of places? Just by travelling all day, our nicely pressed *salwar kameezes* looked dusty and tired! Luckshmi and I looked at each other knowingly.

He came directly towards Les and I, welcoming us with a beaming smile. He insisted we travel with him in his car while the girls followed in the minibus. His car was adorned with a huge assortment of Catholic paraphernalia. We proceeded to the hotel, which he assured us was the best he could get, and because his friend was the owner, we would have the best rooms. Throughout the journey he spoke of the wonderful work he was doing educating children who had no financial help at all. He was especially delightful and gracious to Les who, as trustee of AKIN, was obviously the one that had been supporting his work with the poor. He proliferated his gratitude saying that Gibraltar was the only means of support he received and his own church in India had not helped him at all.

When we arrived at the hotel, he gave us the itinerary for the following day. The driver of the minibus would be our guide and take us to the location of his parish, which was a one-hour drive from the hotel. We said our goodbyes and checked in. We all looked at each other. Something felt wrong. The place looked seedy and several weird looking men loitering in the reception area began staring at us girls. We were shown to our rooms and then agreed to meet back in reception once we had freshened up. Within five minutes of entering my room, the phone rang and I rushed to pick it up thinking it was Luckshmi or one of the team members.

"Hello?"

I was greeted by a thick, slimy accent. "Madam, you like your room?" Then he started sighing heavily as if he was pleasuring himself and it freaked me out! I slammed the phone down.

Les was standing in the doorway. "What's wrong, Nal?" he asked.

I ran towards the door.

"Les, we have to check on the girls." Just as I got to the corridor Chandra came racing towards me saying, "Nalanie, there was a man following me and I feel really uncomfortable."

"Oh, no!" I exclaimed. "Come on, let's check on the others."

We ran to see Shanti, Janaki, Krssy and Luckshmi (Paddy had left us in Coimbatore, as he had to go back to work in the UK). Fortunately, they were fine and had begun to unpack. We called them together and I said, "There is something really sinister about this hotel. I just received a weird phone call. There was a man heavy breathing! And Chandra was just followed by a strange looking man so I think we need to leave

141

immediately. The men here are not used to seeing western women like us, and I don't think it's safe to stay."

The girls agreed so we dragged our suitcases down to the reception desk where we informed the clerk of our decision to check out. We told him we were happy to pay for the first night but he refused. He was very disagreeable and insisted we had to pay for the three nights that had been booked. Shanti and Les went to organize the luggage and call our driver to bring the minibus up front while the rest of us argued with the clerk. We just wanted to settle up and get out of the place. Eventually we got our way and only paid for the first night. We raced to the minibus and decided to tell Father Mabu the following day what had happened and why we left that deplorable hotel.

The driver of the minibus was sympathetic. He consoled us and told us he knew of another hotel that would be perfect for our stay. It was brand new, modern and in a better area. We sighed with relief when we got there; it was indeed perfect! By this time we were all famished so we sat down together for dinner in the nice clean dining room. Exhausted and dusty, we laughed over the day's events and came to the conclusion that none of us trusted Father Mabu. So we devised a plan.

All of us felt as though we were in a movie so we prepared the script for the following day. Les and I would distract Father Mabu while the others were to walk around wherever he was going to take us, the church or a school, and ask whoever we met certain questions designed to either allay our suspicions or to confirm them. Janaki decided she would call Paddy in the UK and let him know where we were staying in case anything should happen to us. Luckshmi and Krssy were especially fired up – we all knew it was really no laughing matter and we needed to be careful. I went to bed praying for everyone's safety. This situation brought Les out of himself, as being the only man in the team he felt the responsibility of having to look after us and was eager to do so. But the girls were feisty and strong, and this created a dynamic energy. We were about to have an adventure and we all felt up to the challenge.

We awoke at the crack of dawn and our driver was already waiting for us in the courtyard. We struck up a conversation with him and he told us he was engaged to be married, and that he was looking forward to his wedding, which was fast approaching. I questioned whether it was an arranged marriage. He replied that he was fortunate that even though it was an arranged marriage he actually fell in love with his wife-to-be.

Now he was working hard to be able to pay for the wedding ceremonies (in the Hindu culture weddings comprise numerous ceremonies spanning several days).

His instructions were to drive us to Father Mabu's parish. En route we sang mantras to pass the time. We were all in good spirits and the dark events of the previous afternoon had disappeared in the light of the new day. And the dawn had brought with it some doubts. Had we exaggerated the severity of the situation? Maybe Father Mabu was really a good guy and had dressed pristinely just to greet us. We were about to find out.

When we arrived at the church there to greet us was Father Mabu and his two 'bodyguards'.

Before arriving in India, Les had emailed Father Mabu to tell him we had collected some funds for him and would bring them to him personally. So as soon as he saw us he invited us straight into his office to receive the donation.

I hesitated and said, "Father Mabu, I want to see your church. Our group would love to say a prayer of thanks for getting here safely."

Reluctantly he took us into the church, which stood just a few metres away from the office building. It was a quaint, small church and modestly decorated but to me it lacked the spiritual vibe. We sat and prayed and from the corner of my eyes I could see that he was very restless. *A man of God? I don't think so,* I told myself. We continued praying quietly and when we finished, we stood up and Les and I went with him back to the office while the girls said they wanted to look around the church and the grounds.

In the office, Father Mabu began explaining to us how he was sent to India following completion of his studies in Rome, and how he had no financial help from anyone except from the donors in Gibraltar. He complained about the bishop of that area saying he feared the bishop was corrupt and that is why he never received any assistance from the church. Then he showed us some school uniforms he had purchased for the school children in his parish, which he claimed had been bought using the donations received from Gibraltar. We then handed him some of the money we had brought with us to pay for more of the uniforms, and books and medical treatments that some of the students apparently required. We held back quite a substantial amount just in case our concerns about his honesty proved founded. I must admit he nearly had Les and I convinced that he really cared for the poor. That was, until we arrived at the next stop, which was the parish school.

The road to the school was uneven and dusty, and one could clearly see the immense poverty this area suffered. The extreme conditions the people living there had to endure were heart-breaking. Many were living in mud or tin huts, which in the summer sweltered with temperatures of over forty-two degrees. I kept repeating a mantra, mentally visualizing light and peace surrounding them.

On arrival, we were welcomed by the headmaster of the school who took us to a classroom where he asked us to sit while the uniforms were presented to the children. We sat down on the cheap plastic chairs laid out for us and observed the children who smiled at us shyly and captivated our hearts. They then proceeded to sing for us as a token of their gratitude. While they were performing, Father Mabu kept talking to Les and myself, telling us of the wonderful work he had done to provide this facility for the children. How the whole village loved him as their saviour. He then began to make defamatory remarks about his bishop again, but this time Les started to record the conversation on his smartphone. We didn't notice he was doing this until he winked at me, as if to say, 'keep him talking'. Unfortunately, when we checked the recording later because of the children singing in the background the conversation was barely audible.

This incident made it obvious that Father Mabu had no interest whatsoever in the children. Earlier, on entering the classroom, we noticed and thought it extremely odd that none of the children greeted him and, even stranger, that he hadn't made any effort to acknowledge them. Les remarked later that he thought it awfully rude of Father Mabu to ignore the children singing and instead preferred to hold a conversation entirely focussed on money and the huge amount he needed in order to perform his God-given work. When the show was over, we walked outside the classroom where Krssy and Luckshmi pointed to a plaque placed on the side of the building and that was engraved with the words 'Donated by the Bishop'. So why was Father Mabu lying and saying the bishop did nothing?

While Father Mabu was conversing with the headmaster, I went to speak with one of the female teachers who I learned could speak English, and I asked her very quietly, "is it true that Father Mabu is funding the school, the teachers and the children?'

She looked at me with fear in her eyes and pleaded, "Please don't tell him I said anything. He never gives us any money. He comes here when foreigners come and he uses our school so they can give him money."

Shocked at this revelation, I asked her, "So why do you let him get away with it?"

"People think that being a priest, we have to listen to everything he tells us to do because in our culture if you answer back to a priest you will have very bad luck, and everyone here is petrified of him and his men." She looked back to see if anyone was watching us. I quickly changed the subject and started speaking about the standard of English the children were taught in the school.

On cue Les approached Father Mabu to further distract him. Just then Chandra came to me with tears in her eyes and was shaking. "Nalanie, the headmaster is hitting the children with his stick to get the them back into the classroom. It's horrible. Come quickly."

I ran up to the headmaster, and with the team by my side, I told him that if he ever dared to hit those children again, we would stop all funding. The headmaster frowned and answered that it was the only way to discipline them. Luckshmi, Krssy, Janaki and Chandra began letting him know, in no uncertain terms, what they thought about his behaviour while Shanti and Les stood next to me to protect me in case a fight broke out.

"Father Mabu," I said sternly. "Tell him to stop this way of teaching forever or we will tell all the donors to cease supporting the school. How dare he treat the children like that! In Europe, he would be arrested."

"Sister Nalanie," he replied, "please don't be upset, I will ask him to stop it." He proceeded to speak to the headmaster in Urdu, which none us understood, after which the headmaster quickly retreated from our sight.

We were then ushered to our transport and driven back to the office building beside Father Mabu's church where lunch was served. The whole situation had become really awkward. We all felt an inner turmoil. We tried to be pleasant to Father Mabu so that he wouldn't guess we had caught on to him. The atmosphere over lunch could be cut with a knife. Yucks! I disliked feeling like a hypocrite intensely. *Nalanie, just act out the part and don't start to get emotional.*

Our next visit was to a doctor who we were told was an expert in Naturopathy and Homeopathy. Father Mabu assured us the doctor was world famous in his field of medicine, and that he had taken it upon himself to care for the villagers. He allegedly charged them a pittance or more than often gave his services free of charge. We were informed the purpose of this visit was because the doctor needed financial help to buy the medical supplies and drugs he needed desperately for his patients.

As we approached the doctor's surgery, we noticed that the area was far different to the one we had just come from. The buildings were of a better construction and the homes appeared to belong to a more affluent class. Les and I again travelled by car with Father Mabu and we arrived ahead of the girls in the minibus. Father Mabu escorted us to meet the doctor. To our surprise his surgery resembled more of a home. There were no patients waiting in the reception room, no nurses and no staff. We were directed into the doctor's office where the walls were adorned with certificates and diplomas. There was something eerie about it all. A doctor who was supposed to be devoted to serving the poor, yet where were the patients? This was India, the reception should have been packed with people! The doctor was, of course, pleased to meet us. I think his brain was seeing dollar signs. He began the meeting by giving us a long dialogue extolling his fame and how people from all over the world came to see him, and because of his humbleness he had chosen to dedicate his life to aiding Father Mabu's great work with the needy. Alas, now he was running out of funds and desperately required our 'kind assistance'.

Just at that moment, Luckshmi ran into the room sobbing. I got up immediately and hugged her. I excused myself and guided Luckshmi out of the room explaining that she had a sensitive nature and seeing the children being beaten that morning had really upset her. We went into the garden where nobody could hear us.

"Nalanie, this is all a scam," she said quietly. "The driver told us that Father Mabu had a group of Germans tourists visiting just last week and they gave him over four thousand Euros. He doesn't support the children at all. He keeps the money for himself and he has a network of people who work with him. Please, you cannot say anything at all otherwise they might harm the driver. He said his life would be in danger if they find out he told us."

"Stay calm," I replied. "We need to be really careful. Thank you for finding this out. I'll speak to the driver* on our way home. Keep cool. We don't want to alert Father Mabu."

I gave her a huge hug and asked her to console the rest of the team who she said were all deeply distressed. I instructed Luckshmi to tell them not to talk with anyone until Les and I concluded the meeting and joined them back at the minibus.

"And don't be concerned, Luckshmi. We will not give them a single penny more." I was upset with myself for having given half the money to Father Mabu that morning. Les did tell me to wait but I got fooled by the sight of all those uniforms he allegedly purchased.

I re-entered the office and again made excuses for Luckshmi's outburst. I informed the doctor that we would go back to the hotel and discuss things and see how we could support him. But I couldn't contain myself and said, "Doctor, I cannot understand one thing. I don't see any patients here. Where are all those people you told me about that need help, why is your reception area empty?"

He twitched nervously and answered, "Madam, you must understand it is afternoon here and too hot for people to come. If you come in the evening you will see crowds."

Les and I looked at each other. We didn't believe him at all. 'Hogwash,' we thought.

*By this time we had become quite friendly with the driver of the minibus who volunteered to inform us about Father Mabu based on what he had personally witnessed. Even today I am reluctant to reveal his name out of concern for his safety.

Before leaving we thanked Father Mabu and made plans to meet him early the following day. We urged him not to organize too much for us, as we needed to be back at the hotel well before dinner in order to discuss everything we had seen and assess to what extent we would be able to help him. We made the excuse that, as trustees of two charities, we needed to seriously consider his requirements and the individual merits of each project he had shown us. On mentioning the word 'hotel', he glared at us and said we had annoyed his good friend tremendously and that he was very insulted by us leaving.

"What could we do, Father Mabu?" I said. "There were strange men staring at the girls and myself and then I had an awful phone call. We did not feel safe there. You need to tell your friend about it, in case it happens to someone else"

We said goodbye to Father Mabu and jumped into the minibus. As we drove away, a cacophony of voices spilt out all the discoveries they had made while Les and I were with Father Mabu.

On hearing the excitement in the team's voices the driver became extremely nervous. "Please madam, please do not say that I told you all this. Father Mabu is not a good man. He takes the money for himself and his men. He has a very luxurious apartment in the city and every night asks me to fetch prostitutes to him. He is bad. Very bad man. Last week he told some German tourists the same story, that no one helped him and he had to use all his own money to help the children, and they believed him."

"Why are you telling us all this?" I asked. "How long have you known him?"

"I saw that your group was different from all the people I drive. You are good people. You pray. You sing Mantras. You hug the poor children. You treat me kindly and offer me food. How can I allow Father Mabu to steal from people like you? God will punish me. But I am scared he will kill me if he finds out. I know Mabu for one year. I got job as driver and I thought I so lucky to have rich boss, as I am getting married and need money. Then I saw how he was cheating everyone, using women and children to get what he wants."

I felt numb. Les felt even worse, as it was his idea to come to Andhra Pradesh. He felt responsible for putting us in jeopardy and was deeply concerned for our safety. As leader of the group I felt I shared this responsibility.

After much discussion and deliberation, I said to the team, "Listen, we have to return tomorrow otherwise Father Mabu will become suspicious and may catch on to the fact that our driver has disclosed everything to us. You girls stay at the hotel and Les and I will go alone."

"No way, Aunty Nal," Krssy responded. "We are all feisty women. If Les and you are going, we will all go! Besides, you need us. We have to gather as much information as possible so that when you get back to Gibraltar you can file a report with the Catholic Church."

None of us slept much that night. Les and I started to talk about our relationship. During this whole episode, he was calm and quiet, and we hadn't spoken about 'us' since Coimbatore when he scolded me for being so unkind to him. Luckshmi and Krssy had witnessed this outburst, and told me I was right to leave him and he had no right to get angry with me. Looking back at all of this, I realize he had every right to get mad with me. I had ganged up with the team and made him feel he was invisible, and that definitely was not kind. I should not have discussed our relationship with anyone. Throughout my married life, Shanky and I never discussed our problems with anyone preferring instead to solve them internally, within our small family. Further, my advice to my clients was always not to discuss personal problems with too many people, as they would more often than not get distorted viewpoints, each coming from their own perception of life. And there I was going against my own advice. Everyone means well, but because of their love for me, their views towards Les had become biased instead of neutral, and I had lost my balance and was no longer staying firm in my convictions and resolving my own issues.

That night at the hotel I admitted all this to Les and told him that I needed time alone to return to my balanced state. It was nothing to do with him. I just was not ready to give up my peace for anyone. He was very hurt but still treated me with respect, and was sincerely worried about my safety during this 'Father Mabu' episode. He said he would make sure he was by my side constantly and do what he could to protect me. However, he continued, because our team was endowed with strong, determined women, they had taken over the role of protectors and that made him feel irrelevant. We had mistaken his silence for weakness. Shanti, thank God, was the only one who supported him.

The conversation that night softened my attitude towards him and I again felt love for him. He sensed it and felt it wasn't the end. I answered it would never be the end of our friendship unless he chose it, but we could not be lovers.

The dawn brought a new challenge, and we were prepared. Armed with knowledge and faith in Divine protection, we prayed for wisdom, understanding and strength.

We arrived at Father Mabu's office where he was waiting for us. Sitting on the benches outside was a group of impoverished looking people from the area. Father Mabu received us with a huge smile and told us he had organized for some of the families being supported by our charity to be there so that we could personally hand them the donations we had left with him the day before. Amongst the group of villagers was a sweet young girl we took to be in her late teens, and who looked sad and uneasy. She would not look up at Les and I as we handed her the money. I asked her to give me a hug, wished her well and told her to get a good education and promote women's rights in India. She looked up with tears in her eyes. On seeing her reaction, Father Mabu quickly ushered us into his office. We left the team outside to snoop around and see what else they could find out about Father Mabu. They were brilliant! They challenged the men to a game of football. Men vs women. I felt sorry for the men.

Father Mabu again gave Les and I a long speech about his difficult work and how many sacrifices he has made for 'these poor forlorn people'. In response I quoted Mother Teresa to him, telling him what joy it gave her to serve the poor. I talked to him of the great Yogic principles of truthfulness and non-violence. I told him I did not believe in the divisions that religion created but rather in the unification of mankind. God for me was Love and God was everywhere, in all of us and in the poorest of the poor. It was our duty to look after our earthly brothers and sisters.

"Ah," he said. "I have arranged for you all to meet a great Swami this afternoon. After learning how much you love Yoga, I thought you would love to meet him. He runs an ashram nearby and also does much good work. You see, I think like you. I am different from many of my colleagues. So now, what about the rest of the money you mentioned that you were going to donate? You can see we are in desperate need."

There was nothing else I could do but keep up the pretence to avoid arousing his suspicions, so I lied. "Les and I were concerned about bringing so much cash to India, so what we have decided to do is to transfer the rest of the money to your bank account when we arrive home. As I told you yesterday, we're going to discuss everything when we get back to the hotel this evening and we'll be in touch when we get back to Gibraltar."

Poor guy, he did not know how to answer! We went outside to tell the team that we were going to be served lunch at the church. Chandra came up to me and whispered, "Nalanie, the young girl you gave the money to says it's all an act. She has to return the money to him after we leave this afternoon. She is petrified of Father Mabu and his men. She said they do horrible things to people who don't obey them. Please do not say anything to Father Mabu. We promised her we would keep what she said secret."

I looked at the girl who stood a few metres away and saw that she was crying and trembling.

Chandra continued, "What shall we do?"

"We will talk about it when we are on our own." My mind was racing to come up with a plan of action that wouldn't arouse Father Mabu's suspicions. "I will ask if we can give the girl a lift home in the minibus and make the excuse that I want to find out about her college studies. I will ask Les to go with Father Mabu in his car while I go with you. He wants to take us to meet a Swami this afternoon but I don't know where his ashram is. I just hope the girl lives in the same direction! Stay focussed and calm."

"There's something else." Chandra glanced around to ensure no one was nearby. "When we were playing football at one point the ball rolled into a shed next to the fence and I went inside to retrieve it. Nalanie, there was a brand new motorbike in there and I think it must be one of the most expensive bikes in India. Luckshmi took a photo of it with her phone while the men weren't looking. We'll show you later."

Chandra's husband, Phil, owned a motorbike business in Gibraltar so she was quite familiar with the different makes and models. If she said it was expensive then I had no reason to doubt her. I said I looked forward to seeing the photo later and we both headed for lunch.

Lunch was served by Father Mabu's 'bodyguards', who looked grim and slimy and made us all feel nauseated so we hardly ate anything. We excused ourselves by explaining the extreme heat had made us lose our appetites. I nudged Les under the table and said, "Father Mabu, I hope you don't mind. I have asked that lovely girl we sponsor if we could give her a lift back to her home on our way to the Swami's ashram. I just want to find out more about her and her studies. She seems such a sweet girl. Les, would you mind going in Father Mabu's car while I go with the girls?"

Les smiled knowingly and played along. "Sure! No problem. I can spend time with Father Mabu going over the finances and get more information for our meeting this evening." That made Father Mabu smile. I think he was glad to get rid of this strong, dogmatic woman for a while!

I must say, I felt more exhilarated than fearful. To catch a thief and expose him would be my pleasure! We piled into the minibus and the young girl reiterated what she had told Chandra. Janaki was fuming and we all understood the dilemma we were in. There was nothing we could do as long as we remained in Father Mabu's domain. It was clear now that the gentle and caring priest was in reality the head of a criminal gang who extorted money from unsuspecting charities and kindly tourists. Aside from the two 'bodyguards' and four or five other men we had seen hanging around the church compound, we had no idea as to the exact number of cohorts in his gang or what they were capable of. As long as we played along they kept smiling at us and being polite, but if Father Mabu knew that we were on to him then the pleasantries would surely end and heaven knows what would happen next. He and his army of thugs held the reins so we just had to be patient and keep up the pretence. The Yogic tenet of 'adapt, adjust and accommodate' came to mind. We must make it up as we go along.

Reluctantly, we left the young girl outside her home. Sadness filled our hearts, and frustration and helplessness set in. If only we could take her with us so that she would be safe. We gave her some money and told her not to say anything to Father Mabu.

Everything was very quiet as we entered the ashram. In India, ashrams are usually filled with activity, with many *ashram-ites* going about their various duties. Not here. Where was everyone? Father Mabu and Les were waiting for us and guided us to the Swami's residence. We were ushered into a poorly lit and gloomy room, and a few moments later the Swami entered. Instead of looking peaceful, warm and friendly his sombre demeanour reflected the glum atmosphere in the room.

As he greeted us, we sensed a falseness about him. *Beware of wolves in sheep's clothing,* I told myself. He asked one of his disciples to bring chairs for all of us and started to talk about his work at the ashram and the school he had developed there to provide education for the children in the village.

After listening to so many of Father's Mabu's grandiose lies, I felt compelled to ask the Swami, "Can we please see the school you run here in the ashram? And where are all the *ashram-ites*?"

"Many are resting now," he replied. "Yes, I will ask my disciple to take you to the school after we all have some tea. Father Mabu informed me that your group has been helping him and you all may consider helping us here too?"

We hadn't discussed helping the Swami, so his remark came as a surprise. Thinking about it now, it shouldn't have been so surprising. Adapt, adjust and accommodate. What next, I wondered?

"Well, Swamiji," I said. "We first need to see the school and find out what the needs of the children are. We have all studied the Yoga Sutras of Sri Patanjali and follow the ethics of *yama* and *niyama*. Our charity is called 'Service in Satchidananda' and as you already know, *Satchidananda* means 'truth, knowledge, bliss'. Everything we donate is given with these principles in mind. We admire people like Gandhi and Mother Teresa, and we want to follow in their footsteps. What do you think, Swamiji?"

"Very good, very good," he answered, his head nodding from side to side. He glanced at Father Mabu who was looking decidedly uncomfortable!

The polite and frequently insignificant conversation continued for a few minutes, and then we were escorted to where the school was located, which curiously was quite a distance away from the main ashram building. There we at last found some form of activity. There was a young man teaching a small group of teenage boys. Everything looked quite legitimate and the teacher was pleasant. He explained that the school received some funding from the United States through the ashram. We stayed a short while and then made our way back to minibus.

"Your train leaves tomorrow at 1pm for Chennai." Father Mabu commented. "I will come to the hotel at 11am to say goodbye".

Les explained to him there was no need, as our driver could take us straight to the railway station. He told Father Mabu not to trouble himself. It was a long way to come just to say goodbye when we could easily say goodbye now. But Father Mabu was adamant. "No, no, I must come, you are my guests and it is my responsibility to make sure you make it to the station safely and on time. It is Indian custom."

On our way back to the hotel, our driver informed us that the Swami was part of Father Mabu's gang, and that many times Father Mabu had told him to take prostitutes, alcohol and drugs to the Swami's residence. He went on to say that many Americans had visited the ashram and donated funds thinking that the Swami was a sincere and holy man.

This made our blood boil! Again and again on this pilgrimage we had come across people using the name of God, religion and even children for their own greed, lust and egotistical tendencies. In fact, the sincerest people we had encountered had not mentioned their religious beliefs at all, but rather served for the love of mankind in God's name. Greatly disillusioned, we returned to the hotel, sat down for dinner and discussed the day's events. We had had enough and could not wait to leave. But despite Les's pleas to him, we still had to face Father Mabu one more time.

Les was particularly affected by the events of the last two days, as the Catholic Church in Gibraltar and his charity, AKIN, had been sending funds to Father Mabu for several years. Les said he planned to write a report when he returned to Gibraltar and send it to both the Church and the local police.   With luck the police will contact the Indian law enforcement authorities and action would be taken to stop Father Mabu from ripping off anyone else.   The driver begged Les not to mention his name in the report, or the name of the young girl, as he feared their lives would be put at risk. Les reassured him he would be extremely careful when writing the report and he promised not to mention their names. We all gave him our word we would not implicate them in any way. We decided to give the driver some money towards his wedding and advised him to leave Father Mabu's employment as soon as he could. He said he had thought a lot about it the past few days and had decided he and his fiancée would move elsewhere in India to be as far away as possible from Father Mabu. It was the only way he could be free. If he stayed in Vijayavada, they would hunt him down, as he knew too much about their criminal activities. We applauded him and gave him our details in case he needed any help. He thanked us profusely and said he would take us to the train station the following morning.

Our final day in Andhra Pradesh could not have come quickly enough. Packed and ready to leave, we waited for the driver in the hotel reception. There was no sign of him, and we were becoming anxious. When Father Mabu arrived, we asked if he knew of his whereabouts.

"Oh, he is not coming today. I had another job for him that needed attending to. I have brought two cars with me. I will take some of you in my car and the rest can go in the second car."

We had not expected this. I was praying under my breath, *please, please keep the driver safe!* Les, Shanti, and I took Father Mabu to the coffee shop and offered him a drink before we set off. The other four excused themselves and we found out later that they had given their phone numbers and the license plates of the two cars to the receptionist of the hotel just in case something happened.

Over coffee Father Mabu blurted out that he had expected more money from us, as we had originally assured him we would give him another couple of thousand dollars. He said he had promised the school and the doctor that we would donate funds to them. They both needed supplies urgently so wasn't there something more we could give him just to appease them?

I looked at him. So that's why he was so insistent on taking us to the train station. He wanted one last try to squeeze money from us. "I apologize Father Mabu, but we have given all our cash away while we've been in India. This is our last stop before we head home. What little cash we have we need to pay for our hotel in Chennai."

"You know, what you paid for the minibus was too little. Petrol is expensive here and we had underestimated the costs. We need ten thousand rupees more." (Equivalent to approximately one hundred and twenty Euros)

"You must be joking!" I exclaimed. I had had enough. "I have travelled all of India many times in the past with my father and I know the cost of things here. What you are quoting is extortionate! What do you take me for, Father Mabu? A fool? We cannot and will not pay that! I am surprised that you should even ask that, as we already agreed the price for the minibus and the driver two days before we arrived. We agreed at the meeting last night to support all your projects and to send you more money than you will have expected". I hated lying but I had no choice. "So you can take the extra costs from there if you really need to. Anyway, we need to leave now. We don't want to miss our train."

Les, Chandra and I got into Father Mabu's car. Janaki, Luckshmi, Krssy and Shanti were shown to the other car. As we were about to pull away, Father Mabu said something in Urdu to the driver of the other car. We then set off in convoy. A short while later we arrived at the train station but the girls, who left ahead of us, were nowhere to be seen.

We became alarmed. "Father Mabu, where are the girls? Why are they not here yet? We have twenty minutes to catch our train."

"Don't worry Mr Les," he replied. "You go in first and I will bring them when the car arrives."

In his words, Les then 'lost it'. He no longer cared about the size of the driver of the car we had travelled in or that he was out-numbered two to one. He screamed at Father Mabu, "No! We will not leave until they are here. Call the driver and get the girls here now! If you don't, I promise you I will not send you a single penny. Do you hear me? We want them here right now!"

I must say I was quite impressed, as I had never seen him speak with such force and power! It worked. Father Mabu got on the phone and within ten minutes the second car arrived. During that time, we were praying and praying. Chandra and I were holding on to each other while Les glared at Father Mabu and continued to give him a mouthful.

When the car pulled up we told the girls to run, run fast or we will miss our train. Father Mabu looked at us and told us to go slowly, and that there was no rush. We ignored him and got to the train just in time. Another minute and it would have left without us. We looked down the platform and saw Father Mabu and his two bodyguards smiling and waving at us. Wow! It was just like a scene from a movie! The train was packed and stank of urine but we didn't care. We were on our way. We managed to find just enough seats scattered in the same cabin and we slumped there, sighing with relief. Les sat next to me and put his arms around me. We asked the girls what had happened to them. Why did it take so long for them to get to the railway station.

They said they were taken to the first hotel, the one we refused to stay at, where some of Father Mabu's men were waiting for them. They demanded the girls pay the balance of the money owed to the owner at which point Janaki suddenly got out of the car and screamed at the top of her voice, "If you don't take us to the train station right now, right this minute, I will get the police after you. I left a message at the hotel saying that if we were missing to go and look for Father Mabu!" At that moment, the driver of the car received the phone call from Father Mabu instructing him to take the girls directly to the railway station.

I was just so very grateful everyone was safe. So very grateful that we were protected by a force so powerful. I told the girls how I felt and they all agreed. At the time it was a frightening experience but now, looking back, it was an adventure, a story to tell the grandchildren. We reached Chennai not only thankful to have left Andhra Pradesh but also firm in our resolve to take action against Father Mabu when we returned home to Gibraltar.* We are not vindictive. We just didn't want anyone else to experience what we had been through.

*Les did file a report with both the Catholic Church in Gibraltar and with the Gibraltar Financial Crime Intelligence Unit. However, both organisations insisted on disclosure of the names of the driver and the young girl, which we were not prepared to reveal. As a result, neither the Catholic Church nor the Gibraltar Police took any action whatsoever, and Father Mabu remained at liberty to continue his criminal activities.

Our time in India came to a close the following evening. We parted ways at the airport. Krssy and I were flying to Hong Kong to see our family and the others were heading back to Europe. Going through the myriad experiences we shared during the last two weeks had brought us close together. We said our goodbyes and I looked at Les and told him I hoped we would remain friends. He looked at me with dull eyes and whispered, "Not sure, Nal. Not sure about any of it. I'm in a lot of pain right now and it really hurts."

On the flight to Hong Kong, I had much to digest. Loss, life and love all mingled together in the spinning wheels of my mind. I had lost faith in religion and especially in men who claimed to be holy. I was saddened that India, a country with such incredible spiritual knowledge and beauty, had given birth to so many corrupt men.

Sadly, Father Mabu was not unique. Yet, simultaneously, I felt such warmth to know that people like Papa Vidyaakar, Senthil, Mr Ramaswamy, Uma, Kanchana, Balu, Dr. Thilikavathy and Kartikeyan existed. People who were charged with a holy force. Their force was not in their words but in their actions.

I was happy and full of gratitude to Paddy, Janaki, Shanti, Krssy, Luckshmi, Chandra and Les for partaking in this amazing journey with me. At the same time I was sad that I had caused pain to someone I truly loved. I realized that I still had much to learn and grow. I felt India had matured me in many ways. Its ugliness became my ugliness. Its beauty became my beauty. India had revealed my weaknesses. Who was I? Who truly was Nalanie? Shanky had left me so I could grow to be a better person, to have time to evolve my personality. Not to be shadowed by the needs of others but to strive forward in serving mankind in my small way. I felt humbled by life and the enormity of Spirit. I sighed and meditated all the way to Hong Kong.

'The teacher who walks in the shadow of the temple, among his followers, gives not of his wisdom but rather of his faith and his lovingness.

If he is indeed wise, he does not bid you enter the house of his wisdom, but rather leads you to the threshold of your own mind.

The astronomer may speak to you of his understanding of space, but he cannot give you his understanding.

The musician may sing to you of the rhythm which is in all space, but he cannot give you the ear which arrests the rhythm, nor the voice that echoes it.

And he who is versed in the science of numbers can tell of the regions of weight and measure, but he cannot conduct you thither.

For the vision of one man lends not its wings to another man.

And even as each one of you stands alone in God's knowledge, so must each one of you be alone in his knowledge of God and in his understanding of the earth.'

Kahil Gibran

Chapter 3
Manna From Heaven

Being with family in the luxury of the Harilela home was a tonic and the rest I needed after India. It was great to feel pampered and not to deal with housework, laundry, accounts and appointments.

The Harilelas firmly believed in a 'joint family' system; all under one roof. The family home was a 52-bedroom mansion where my father and his five brothers and their sister all lived together. The home was divided into separate apartments per family and on the ground floor we shared the communal swimming pool, library, kitchen, lounge, party and dining rooms. Every Sunday evening the whole family would gather for cocktails and dinner, which would also include any guests, be they extended family, friends or business associates. I loved those Sunday dinners! We are an extremely close family and it was my Dad's wish before he passed away that we should always maintain the tradition.

Living in separate apartments, albeit in the same home, and all leading busy lives, left little time for communication between the families especially during the working week. So Dad entreated us to keep in contact at least for Sunday dinners so that the closeness and the unity of the family would not be lost. When he was alive, my Dad was the *Guru* of the family - the spiritual head and heart - and he filled those Sunday dinners with song, laughter and gratitude. He would never miss an opportunity to thank God for all the family has received. This served to remind us all not to take life for granted.

Now I was home again, but it wasn't the same. I missed Dad. I missed his loving energy. I felt a kinship with Mom after losing Shanky and spent most of my days with her in her apartment. Siblings, cousins and friends would invite me out for dinner, but instead I would request we stayed home with Mom. I lost all interest in large social gatherings and refused many invitations.

My beautiful sister Mira arranged for me to give a talk at the family hotel, *The Holiday Inn Golden Mile*. I was touched that my elder sister was so proud of me, and that she wanted me to share whatever spiritual knowledge I had with her friends and the general public. Every time I visited Hong Kong, Mira would ask me if I wouldn't mind giving a talk and, of course, I always said yes. So she would take care of all the advertising and the organisation, tasks she was extremely good at as evidenced by the regular good attendances. I loved every opportunity to share spirit whenever and wherever I was invited to speak! Just being in the company of like-minded people elevated my spirits and when I felt theirs lifted as well, it just gave and still gives me so much joy! What else can we do in this life? Everything comes to a 'dead end' and I feel so strongly in my heart that everyone deserves to be joyful. We need to be taught how to deal with sorrow and tragedies and to show that it is possible to surf the wave of suffering when you are armed with the right knowledge. We all die. The real problem lies in the fact that too many do not live peacefully. As someone once famously said, 'Do not fear dying but rather fear not living well!'

What can I tell you about my grandchildren? Indira and Shahan again showed me the reason for continuing life. Watching their growth, their curiosity, their innocence and their pure honesty. This 'aliveness' and *joie de vivre* should be the way we live throughout our entire lives but as we grow older we become more cynical and gradually lose the light we were born with and manifested as children.

Looking at Shahan, I saw Shanky and my heart ached for what he had missed. Or was he watching from the other side? Shaman was settling well in Hong Kong but I still sensed a deep sadness in him. We spent a lot of time talking but I knew that this was a journey I could not take for him. Patience, I told myself, life and time heals all. He spent every available moment with me after finishing his work to make sure I was alright. His strength and protection of me gave me solace as a mother and made me feel proud that he was so caring. I strongly believe that our children come to us on loan, and as parents we are their caretakers and guides. Ownership does not come into it. They are a gift to us.

As a young teenager, I came across the book *The Prophet* by Kahil Gibran, and it made a huge impression on me. I remember so clearly when my children were born and throughout their childhood, I kept reminding myself that they are on loan to me, and my responsibility is to love, nurture and guide them. Not to own them.

"Your children are not your children.
They are the sons and daughters of Life's longing for itself.
They come through you but not from you.
And though they are with you yet they belong not to you.
You may give them your love but not your thoughts,
For they have their own thoughts.
You may house their bodies but not their souls,
For their souls dwell in the house of tomorrow, which you cannot visit
Not even in your dreams."

(*On Children* - From *The Prophet* by Kahil Gibran)

During my visit to the family home, I received a call one evening from Dada Hari, my father's brother, asking me to join him for dinner in his apartment. Dada was an impressive man, highly intellectual and I was in awe of his aura.

"Nalanie, I heard from Krssy that the charity you formed is involved in aiding multiple projects for people in need. I know that your father would be very proud of you. She also mentioned that you have bought a house in Spain where you plan to build a Yoga Hall. Is that right? How do you expect to pay for it?"

"Dada, I had thought to do exactly as I did with the Gibraltar Yoga Centre. I will give talks and collect donations, and build the Centre brick by brick."

"Do you have any idea of how much it may cost?"

"Yes, I actually had the architect give me an estimate. He said it would cost approximately eighty-two thousand Euros."

"It may take you a long time to raise those funds," he rightly pointed out. "I have a better idea. I will pay for it but I have two conditions. The first is that you name the hall after your father; call it 'George Harilela Hall.' The second is that you have to be the sole owner and run it independently from any other organization."

My jaw dropped! I could not believe what I was hearing. "Dada, I don't know what to say! I am flabbergasted by your offer. It's such a lot of money. Thank you is all I can say, and yes, of course I agree with your conditions!"

He smiled, "This is what your father would have wanted. I am sure, if he was alive, he would have built it for you."

Following dinner, I rushed to tell Shaman the great news. He hugged me and told me how happy he was for me. I asked him to help me think of a name for my new home. I was thinking along the lines of a Sanskrit name, but nothing sounded right. Nothing came to us that evening but a few days later Shaman asked me, "Mom, what about a Spanish name?"

"No, I don't think so, but what did you have in mind?" I replied.

"*Casa Bella Vida*", he said, "which means *Home of a Beautiful Life*. What do you think?"

I stared at him profoundly and surprised myself by saying, "It's perfect. I believe we should all live beautiful lives!" And *Casa Bella Vida* became the name of my home.

I think I was in a daze for the rest of my stay in Hong Kong. I marvelled at the Divine plan. Everything that was required just materialized miraculously in such a short space of time. I could see scriptural truths evolve in front of me. I experienced the deep joy in knowing that Consciousness was there watching my back so long as I danced with life through the good and bad times. When something so positively Divine occurs, I notice that my meditations naturally intensify, ideas stream through my mind as if the Gods are speaking to me, guiding me to do quickly that which has already been ordained. The floodgates of inspiration and love infiltrate every cell in my body, so much so that my 'being' is fed with such an energy that causes the *chakras** to play as I lie on my bed at night.

* See Appendix

163

I feel the churning in my body and I know - without knowing - that I am being healed. This is an awe-inspiring experience that makes me feel blissed out and extremely grateful. Whenever it happens, it charges my resolve and spurs me forward in a new direction. Flowing through the horrendous pain of the loss of a loved one and accepting it by surrendering totally creates fluidity in the mind, which lessens its grasping aspects. One's thoughts and emotions become like water.

Water is fluid, soft and yielding
But water will wear away rock,
Which is rigid and cannot yield.
As a rule, whatever is fluid, is soft
And yielding will overcome whatever
Is rigid and hard.
This is another paradox:
What is soft is strong.

(Lao Tzu From *The Tao Te Ching)*

Ideas flowed through my mind and I was eager to return home to set the wheels in motion. I was eager to inform the *sangha* and demonstrate that indeed 'faith could move mountains', and that manna came from heaven. And where was heaven? Right here, right now, in the moment. And all the hardness I experienced washed into a glow of hope and light.

Although I was in high spirits and excited to return to Spain, I learned that as a result of our break-up Les had become withdrawn and moody. Despite the ostensible closeness we tried to engender between us in India he still felt extremely hurt, and found it difficult to come to terms with our separation. In particular, during the time I was away in Hong Kong, his moodiness had degenerated to the point where he began to think that seeing me again would be too painful for him to bear. He had become so upset that, following my return, every Wednesday when I was in Gibraltar for my regular *satsangs* at the Yoga Centre he would make a determined effort to avoid those parts of the town where he knew I would be. Over the time we had been together, he had become familiar with my Wednesday routine so he was acutely aware of the time and the route I would take to go to the Yoga Centre, which invariably required me to pass his office situated on the main street. He often had to attend his clients' offices in other parts of the town and, when he did, he always tried to time such visits so as not to coincide with my passing by, or else take a circuitous route to avoid bumping into me. However, the gods had other ideas and neither of us could believe the number of times we came across each other in the street. At first he walked by without saying a word and wouldn't even look at me, which I thought extremely childish of him!

However, on one particular occasion, when we again met each other despite his efforts to avoid me, he stopped me and asked if I had anything to say to him. He appeared confused by the perplexed look on my face, and asked me to call him later, and then turned to walk away. At the time I was in conversation with one of the Yogis I had just met in the street and she called after him that *he* should call *me*, not the other way around. And that evening he did just that, and the story he told me made me laugh!

A few days earlier had been Valentine's Day and, in an effort to win back my heart he purchased a bunch of yellow roses, which he knew were my favourite flowers. Then, very early in the morning, he drove to my home in Sotogrande and dropped the roses over the wall into my driveway. Having accomplished his surreptitious mission he quickly drove away and expected me to call him to ask if he had sent the roses, as there was no note attached, and to thank him. When he hadn't received the anticipated phone call he became concerned that perhaps I hadn't appreciated the flowers were from him, and this prompted his question to me when we met in the street.

Unfortunately, however, I had to tell him there were no roses on my driveway on the morning of Valentine's Day, and we both wondered what had happened. His ploy to rekindle my love for him had failed, and in a way that mystified us both. Had someone come to my house and stolen the bunch of roses? What had gone wrong? Then it dawned on me. Just prior to Valentine's Day I had taken delivery of some furniture and left the large packing boxes they came in leaning against the wall on the driveway. As the wall was quite high Les could not see the boxes on the other side and so he had inadvertently dropped the roses directly into one of them. Later that day the boxes were taken away to be disposed of - and with the roses still hidden inside!

It appeared that, on this occasion, the gods didn't want me to receive the roses (the absence of a note rendered the ploy too nebulous to be effective) and instead, possibly through some mischief on their part, they preferred the incident should result in a more positive outcome, that of sparking conversation between us again. And the conversation was light. We both laughed but it still took a while before we got back together.

Chapter 4
Bricks And Mortar

As soon as I landed back in Spain, I was thrown into meetings with my architect and builders. There were walls to come down and rooms to be extended. Plumbing, electrics, doorframes, a new kitchen; it was both daunting and exciting. My days were so full with driving up and down to check the building works, giving courses, seeing patients, receiving visitors, spending time with family and *sangha* members. I look back now and wonder how I attended to it all. As I said earlier, there was an energy greater than me that pushed me forward. The secret, I realized, was to make quick decisions when working with the builders. We can look around forever for better offers on materials. I made it very simple for myself when choosing tiles for floors, doors, windows and everything else. I stuck to the budget. No matter how much I preferred another tile or piece of furniture, I refused to go over budget. Sticking to that rule while being sensible about quality helped me through the daily chore of decision-making.

I found myself missing Les's company and thinking about Shanky all the time, and how wonderful it would have been if he were with me to build this home. I also realized that perhaps if he were alive, I would not have purchased this particular house, as he was far more practical than I was and would have commented that it was too old and required an enormous amount of restoration. His dream was always to own a penthouse apartment, which we had already experienced and loved in Gibraltar before we sold it. Andrew helped whenever he could but was too busy sorting out his own business and looking after the family. I was pleased with myself for not falling into victim mode and bewailing, *'I am all alone, there is no one to help me,'* although I will admit I was tempted to a few times! Instead, I repeated to myself those words of wisdom I had been teaching others for years; *'This opportunity is given to me to expand my knowledge, to become more independent, to grow stronger and trust myself more. God is with me; I am not alone.'* The constant repetition of these powerful words kept me going and turned what would have been a terribly stressful ordeal into a tolerable one.

One evening I was walking along the boulevard by the beach when I received a phone call from Nuria, one of my students. Her sister, Coral, had been in hospital for several months battling cancer and now Nuria was calling to say her condition was worsening and the situation had become extremely dire. She asked if I could visit Coral and talk to her to prepare her for what now seemed imminent. I answered that, of course, I will go and see her and I made plans to go to the hospital the following day.

As I stared at the waves crashing against the shore, once more I was reminded of the fragility of life. How transient everything was. Nothing is permanent. Life and death are like the waves breaking against the shoreline and dissolving back into the sea. I understood we would all dissolve back into Consciousness, and it was only a matter of time.

I forced myself out of the reverie and realized I had to inform Les. It had been months since we had spoken and I knew he was close to Coral, so I would have been extremely selfish not to call and let him know she was losing her battle and didn't have much time left. Before I could over-think the matter, I dialled his number and he answered immediately.

"Thank you for letting me know. I would love to see her. I know how much you dislike driving to Marbella so can I pick you up and we can go and see her together?"

"I would love that," I replied. "I've missed your friendship and it would be great to catch up."

"Me too," he answered. "I missed you a lot."

My heart was pounding and I felt the excitement of seeing him again well up in me. I was both surprised at and fearful of my reaction. The following day could not come fast enough. 'Oh no,' I thought. 'Not again! I feel like a teenager! I thought I was over him!'

As his car came into view, I broke out into a huge smile as a feeling of warmth filled my heart. As I jumped into the passenger seat, he kissed my cheek and it was as if we had never parted. We chatted and laughed all the way to the hospital, speaking about trivia and avoiding the subject of *us*. It was a completely different scenario on our way home after the visit.

Coral's health had indeed deteriorated. Both her feet were badly swollen and had a bright purplish hue. It looked as though gangrene had set in. Would they have to amputate? My heart skipped a beat and I wanted to cry so badly. Instead I put on my bravest face, asked her what the doctors had said and spoke candidly to her. Her parents and Nuria were beside her so I gently asked if they wouldn't mind leaving us alone so that I could speak to her openly, and she could talk to me without worrying about upsetting them. Les escorted them out because he understood the need for privacy at this extremely delicate time.

After they left the room, I asked Coral if she feared death, and what her thoughts were. She looked at me sorrowfully and told me that she was not ready to die but the odds were stacked against her. Amputation may buy her a little time but the doctors thought it would be too traumatic. The cancer had metastasized. The treatment was no longer working. Her medical insurance had run out and they had to move her to a public hospital but she was adamant she did not want to move and die there. She was concerned for her daughter, who was only a teenager and, because Coral was estranged from her husband, she didn't have a father to turn to.

I attempted to allay her fears by talking about energy and spirit. I reminded her that the soul never dies. Energy moves into different realms of Consciousness. It was of utmost importance to maintain her peace. We meditated and cried together. I persuaded her to talk to her daughter, and to her partner Mario, as they were both terrified at the prospect of death. Everyone was in denial except her sister, Nuria. There were things to sort out for her daughter and she needed to write her will. I told her to prepare for the worst, but at the same time never to give up hope, as we simply do not know what the future holds. Things can suddenly change for the better. She requested that I remain in the room while she talked to them. I agreed and called them in.

It was such a difficult and moving scene. I looked at their pained expressions and their immediate reaction of denial as she spoke the truth. Her daughter told me later that, although her initial reaction was one of anger at the thought of losing her mom, she was actually quite relieved that what she had been feeling and fearing for months was finally voiced and out in the open. I said goodbye and left them alone in the room to process their emotions together.

I was quiet on the way home and Les asked if he could take me out for a meal. I was grateful to have someone I trusted to talk to. That evening saw the revival of our love. We talked openly and truthfully. I explained how I felt about what happened in India. With my work and my love for people, he would need to accept me for who I was. If he wanted to be around me, he would have to love everyone the way I did. And yes, we all have good days and bad days, but I just couldn't deal with his morose face and depressed moods. There were so many people much worse off than us, and I felt he did not have a right to complain just because he was not receiving the attention he wanted. He remarked it took two hands to clap (I always quoted that in my lectures) and that I needed to look at the attitude I had towards him in India. I told him he was absolutely right. I knew there were issues I needed to sort out if we were to carry on being together, but there were certain things that I would never compromise, not for him or for anyone. Peace was and remains my God, and I had decided not to let anyone or anything disturb it at that stage in my life. I was truly sorry that my mantra of 'adapt, adjust, accommodate' was not just about one particular individual, but rather about service for mankind generally. I had already done a lot of that with my late husband and I was just too old to start again. I told him I was not ready and did not want to hurt him again. After the heavy conversation was out of the way, we laughed and talked and arranged to visit Coral again in the following days.

We returned to the hospital three days later and found Coral in an upbeat mood. She showed me a photograph of a model wearing red boots in the magazine she was glancing through and said, "In my next life, I will own a pair of red boots like these because it is obvious that I won't be able to wear them in this one." And she stared at her feet with an expression of acceptance.

Coral left our world two days later, one day before she was to be moved to the public hospital. She got her wish.

This was quite a hectic period in my life. I was running a teacher-training programme and dear Shanti staffed me as a volunteer. She told me that she felt it was now her duty to look after me and so from that day onwards she started travelling and staffing me wherever I went. Shanti added some comedy to our lives, as she would often blurt out odd things at totally the wrong times. Her eccentricity made us all laugh and she loved that she did that! Poor girl, I had to reprimand her a lot.

She used to carry several bags to every meeting full of things she felt she needed but everyone thought it was all for me and I had asked her to carry so much gear around. One day one of the students questioned why I did that to Shanti so I showed the things that I needed, which were simply my handbag and the book I was teaching from, and the microphone and portable amplifier I had to use in order to save my voice (I invariably had to speak for over an hour, sometimes several sessions in a day so the portable amplifier was an essential so that I didn't have to strain my vocal chords). All the other things Shanti brought, such as the hot water thermos, the cushions, the blanket, the food stuff and extra shawls, were nothing to do with me, they were all for her. That evening I scolded her for bringing so many things, which were solely to make her feel secure, and for telling everyone they were all for me. Hadn't she learnt from travelling with me that we were always provided with whatever we needed by our hosts? After that, she tried hard and eventually succeeded in reducing the load to half! Shanti was always, and continues to be, so gracious with any advice I give her, as she now knows that I am only interested in her wellbeing. Today she is an amazing soul albeit she still has her eccentricities!

Later that year I travelled to Cornwall where I taught a Raja Yoga Foundation Course which I had created and tailored so that anyone and everyone could learn these golden tools, live by them and share them. In five and a half days I tried to share as much as I could. It was quite intensive not only for everyone but also for me. As I watched them shed many layers of fear and psychological baggage it gave me a sense of fulfilment. It was during this course that I became very close to Janaki and her husband Paddy, both extremely generous souls. Janaki, a real gem, maintains a sincere desire to serve and love all; she revealed herself to be a prime example of yoga in action. It is so easy for people to quote spiritual truths, anyone can do that, but when you observe people living by them it is evident they will impart the teachings to many merely by their actions. Actions truly speak louder than words. She loved networking and shared her knowledge freely and lovingly with everyone.

'A wise person will not disturb the mind of an unwise person who is still attached to the fruits of his or her actions. But by continuously performing perfect (selfless actions) the wise influences others in all they do.'

(Living Gita: Chapter 3, Sloka 26)

In Gibraltar, the *sangha* was becoming quite strong and many of my students travelled with me whenever and wherever I was asked to speak or teach a Raja Yoga course. Everyone fell in love with the members of our team, as they were always so kind and considerate of others. Most of all they carried this vibrant energy and exhibited the essence of true *bhakti yoga* - so full of love, and no fear of openly displaying their love.

Love was blossoming in all directions and I came to truly understand that 'the Lord of Love' lives in the hearts of all. When you awaken yourself to this inner power station of love, miracles can unfold.

I was now longing for the Yoga hall to be ready at my new home, so that I wouldn't need to travel so much. I reasoned that if people needed me, they could now come to our new *George Harilela Hall* - or 'GHH' for short. At least, that's what I thought! Until it was ready, I had to continue travelling, mainly to Gibraltar and Marbella, in order to share this incredible science of Yoga with anyone who wished to receive it. Many times, Les would join me and the other students but I was still cautious and avoided getting too close to him. My heart and head were still locked in a struggle. I felt vulnerable but, at the same time, I couldn't stop loving him.

The building work on *Casa Bella Vida* was proceeding but not without its problems. There were a few glitches but they did not disturb me, as they seemed really quite trivial compared with the loss of my darling Shanky. I felt like a surfer riding the waves. The home was slowly taking shape and I enjoyed shopping for it. This was the home God gave me and I could do it up any way I liked! I began to love this feeling of independence and freedom. I walked around the bricks and mortar daily thanking the Divine Consciousness for everything. It was truly phenomenal to watch the Creator's plan take shape and observe myself as the instrument used to put it together. Thinking like this dissolved all the pressure that came with decorating and moving home. And the *sangha*, they were amazing! A group of eleven of them showed up to sort out my beautiful garden. As I watched them all working so hard in the heat of the afternoon I saw in them a host of angels in the form of human beings, and I thanked my beloved Shanky for sending all of them - and Les, who was there alongside everyone else cutting down all the weeds and clearing out all the dead plants. Whenever, we caught each other's eyes, we would just smile at each other.

One of the team was only six years old. Her name was Emmylou and despite the heat of the day she refused to stop and rest. As I watched her pressing her hands into the soil and watering the plants, her face beaming with a sweet innocent smile, I became entranced by the beauty of the scene, her tenderness towards the plants and the way she was so at home with nature. She knew nothing of gardening and yet she worked instinctively, lovingly, happily. Her selfless actions and her demeanour that day affected me deeply, and I was reminded that children are precious gifts sent to teach us. As we grow older and leave childhood behind we often forget to look at the world as we did in our youth: to look at nature with wonder, with excitement. As Dick Van Dyke once said, 'childhood was a wonderful place. I wish I had never left.'

When the work was finished by late evening, the team celebrated and congratulated each other on a job well done. As we surveyed the garden a feeling of contentment welled up and I was reminded of another *Sutra* from *The Yoga Sutras Of Patanjali*:

> *'By contentment, supreme joy is gained.'*

> (Book 2: Sutra 42)

That summer Shaman, Hersha and the children came to visit and we rented a beach house near Shani's so that we could all be together. I loved the days with the family, watching them grow, laugh, play, sing and dance all day. The grandchildren would frequently entertain us by performing shows that they themselves would create. Then one day, while the family were all together, Les called me and said that he had two tickets to a private viewing of the film *The King's Speech,* the screening of which was part of the buildup to the Marbella Film Festival. He knew that it was one of the films I really wanted to see but, so far, I had not had the opportunity to do so. His invitation to join him at the screening was hard to resist, so I said yes, I would love to. I asked Shaman and Shani what they thought about my accepting the invitation and they replied that I needed to do what felt right for me. They just wanted to see me happy.

It seemed the Universe was again conspiring to bring us together. Of all the films that could have been shown as a precursor to the Festival, and that Les was offered tickets to, it had to be the one movie I really wanted to see! We enjoyed the film immensely and again felt that strong chemistry between us. I couldn't understand what was happening to me. My mind and heart seemed once more at odds. I really did not want to play with his emotions but I couldn't help enjoying his company. That night when he left me at my home, we decided we would meet again after Shaman, Hersha and the children had departed back to Hong Kong, as I wanted to spend time as much time as possible with them while they were with us.

So slowly, slowly we started dating again. We were becoming intimate again and we spent many evenings together discussing life and spirit. He admitted to me that he was really upset at God when we had split up, as he couldn't understand how something so wonderful could be given and then taken away so suddenly. I answered that God had nothing to do with it. It was my decision and if he needed to be angry at anyone, it should be me. I had made the decision to break up because I was simply not ready to commit to a permanent relationship. He had too much baggage, and my goal was to retain my peace. I told him that if he loved me, he would just have to be patient and accept that I just wasn't sure. Why couldn't we just take our time and enjoy the moment? It took him some time to digest and accept that this was the way I felt.

But then fate worked its magic to keep us together once more. The contract for the apartment he had rented expired and would not be renewed so he was forced to move out. He located an alternative apartment in a small town just ten minutes away by car from my new home. In the meantime, he was very busy with his work in Gibraltar and curiously had arranged to travel to see his family in the UK in September on the exact dates I was moving into *Casa Bella Vida*.

September 10th arrived. The day I moved into my new home. After the move was complete, I finally had the luxury of sitting down and reflecting in the silence. I recalled that as a child I had a vision that one day I would be living in a house with a garden. When I was thirty years old I bought a 'Portmeirion' teaset and I told my husband it was for the house with a garden that I had envisioned. Not only was there now a house with a garden but it also had a Yoga hall attached to it! How did it all happen with my small budget? Would I be able to keep it with all the expenses that come with a big home? And I stared at the sky and smiled and said, "Divine grace, you have performed miracles for me. One after the other. How can I ever doubt and worry about this? You have built it and you will look after it. I am just your caretaker. If I have to sell it, I will. It is all a gift. Nothing is mine. All is on loan."

I don't know how long I sat there with tears filling my eyes and deep gratitude to the Divine in my heart. I had finally dropped the feeling of wanting to leave this earth and join Shanky. It was replaced by the realization of all the adventures I would be facing now that I had this beautiful home that had come together with so much love. Every brick seemed to reverberate with the sound of the holy mantra...

Chapter 5
The End Of The Beginning

Curtains and blinds went up, paintings found their places on the walls, kitchen cupboards were stocked and, as the saying goes, 'everything in its place and a place for everything - and all in a flurry of activity filled with laughter amongst friends.

When he returned from England Les could not believe how much was accomplished in such a short space of time. He would come over in the evenings after working all day in Gibraltar to help with whatever bits and pieces needed doing, the small jobs and finishing touches.

Sufficient donations from the talks I had been giving, in both Gibraltar and Marbella, enabled Shanti and I to revel in shopping around for chairs, blankets, cushions and Yoga mats for the new *George Harilela Hall*. It was exhilarating to see the Yoga hall come together, and even more so when in late October *sangha* members arrived for the first *satsang* to be offered there. I could feel the presence of my beloved Gurudeva, my Dad and Shanky, as everything just slotted into place so smoothly. I was excited about this new beginning. A home made for service, a home filled with healing energy that would embrace anyone who walked through the doors. This was the dream I always had, and it felt wonderful - and even a little bizarre - to observe the 'unreal become real.'

Then late one night I awoke with gripping abdominal pains and a tremendous feeling of nausea. I ran quietly to the bathroom so as not to disturb Les who had stayed the night. I was vomiting blood. Trying to remain calm and wondering what could possibly be wrong with me, I decided to take a couple of paracetamols and wait till morning before considering what to do next. There was no point in alarming anyone, I told myself. It could be just some passing thing. I returned to bed but the gnawing pain would not allow me to sleep. Meditation had always worked in the past when I was not well so, gripping my stomach I rocked back and forth to ease the pain, and planned what I would do when morning arrived. Dawn broke after what seemed an eternity, and as soon as I saw Les stirring, I gently shook his shoulders and told him what had happened. He became extremely concerned and asked if I had a local doctor I could call. I replied that Peter Borge had always been my doctor but he was based in Gibraltar. I also told Les that if I had to go to a hospital then I would prefer one in Spain. I then telephoned Shani and asked which doctor in Spain she used and could recommend.

"Mom," she said, "I will make an appointment and pick you up and take you there. Give me an hour to organize everything."

"Shani, how will you manage with the three girls."

'Don't worry Mom. Andrew will take them to school and we will figure it out"

"Let me stay with you and take you to Shani's" Les offered.

"Thank you but no." I replied. "You go to work and sort out what you need to. You don't speak Spanish and I need someone who does. I'll let you know how I get on. I may need your help this evening." His face turned pale with worry and reluctantly, he agreed to go to Gibraltar.

As he was leaving I tried to reassure him. "Don't worry Les, all will be well. These things happen as we get older."

By the time Shani arrived the pain had worsened so she drove me straight to the clinic and we sat down in the waiting area. When the doctor saw my ashen face she immediately beckoned me to her consultation room. As she examined me, her expression revealed her concern, and then she announced it was possibly a problem with my gall bladder and I should be seen by a surgeon as a matter of urgency. She picked up the phone and began making the arrangements. I was so fortunate that the surgeon she called was in a hospital nearby and he agreed to see me at short notice. Everything would be covered by my medical insurance so Shani chauffeured me straight to the hospital. As soon as I signed the registration papers, I was placed in a wheelchair and taken to have a scan, ultrasound and X-ray. On seeing the results of the scan, which arrived extremely quickly, the surgeon informed Shani and I that I would need to stay overnight for observation. The scans had revealed a large cyst in my liver that was pushing against all the organs next to it, and he was concerned that my pancreas was affected. In order to get a clearer picture, he said I needed an MRI scan, which would involve me having to go to a special facility within a small boutique hospital a few kilometres away. In the meantime, the doctor continued, I just needed some painkillers and rest.

Shani called Les and informed him of the situation, and asked if he could pick up some pyjamas and toiletries from home and then stay with me the night at the hospital. I told Shani to please get back to her children but she refused to leave me until Les arrived. I was taken to a private room where a nurse inserted a drip and within half an hour the intensity of the pain lessened and, thoroughly exhausted, I drifted off to sleep. A short while later I awoke to the sight of Les sitting on the edge of the bed and smiling at me. I was so grateful to see him! He stroked my hair and said he knew everything was going to be just fine and indeed it was the following day. The doctor returned bright and early, examined me, gave me the release papers and asked me to call him as soon as I got the results from the MRI, which would probably take between a week and ten days. He went on to say that, depending on the results of the MRI scan, we would probably need to think about surgery to remove the cyst. Les asked the doctor if he knew what had caused the cyst, to which the doctor replied that it was congenital. His only concern was that if the cyst contained parasites, it could be potentially life threatening. He asked if I had recently travelled to any third world countries and, of course I replied that I had. And then my memory jerked back to Shanky's words of warning whenever I travelled overseas for my charity: *'Huns, you don't know what diseases you can get from these places. The people there have no idea about hygiene.'*

As Les was driving me home, I stared out of the car window and contemplated the fragility of life. The trees, the mountain, the sky held untold secrets. Did they know? In a fraction of a second, one's life can be turned totally around. What was to be my fate? Being unafraid of the future was a great blessing to me and as I focused on the present I determined to research about liver cysts online as soon as I got home. Sitting in the car beside Les I felt lethargic, extremely tired and still in great discomfort. But Les was calm - a quality I loved about him - and he gave me space to think.

Against everyone's wishes I decided to continue with my work, leading *satsangs* and classes, and giving consultations. There was no point sitting around and doing nothing until the MRI results arrived. To avoid hearsay, I informed the *sangha* members and my students of my condition, but playing it down so as not to raise any concerns. Even so, one of my students asked me, "Nalanie, what would happen if you should die? You just got back on your feet, built this home and this incredible hall! How can you bear this? Why is God doing this to you?"

Laughing, I replied, "What are you worried about? Soul is not born and soul does not die! My body will be cremated and will transform into ash, and that will leave me free to fly wherever I want. Nothing was ever mine. Everything is on loan. I am just so grateful that I have a chance to enjoy this home even for a short while. And if I die it will go to my children, and that will make me so happy. But who said I was going to die anyway?"

Shaman called me every day to check on me and tried to convince me to go to Hong Kong for the operation. He rightly pointed out I would have so much support from the family there, and they all had live-in Filipino maids who could help. But I had no desire to go to Hong Kong and worry my Mom, and besides, I told him, when one is unwell there is no place like home. The surgeon who was going to operate on me was a good man, and I intuitively knew he would do his best.

When the MRI results eventually arrived, they showed an enlarged cyst of over 13 cm in my liver. The operation was now a matter of fact so we booked a day early in December.

"Doctor, please be honest with me, I want to know all the pros and cons."

"The worst case scenario," he replied, "would be parasites in the cyst and that could be fatal, but I'm confident that's not the case. Looking at the scans, I believe it's a water cyst. I'd like to do keyhole surgery but I won't know if that's an option until we are in the operating theatre. I have complete faith everything will go well, so please don't worry. The only thing is if we don't operate then there is the risk the cyst may burst and, if it does, then the damage will be unrepairable."

Les, who was with me and listening intently to the surgeon, then called Shani and asked her to let the family know the situation. I wanted to know more so I contacted Peter Borge who, as my doctor and friend for so many years was concerned for my wellbeing, and asked his opinion whether I really needed the operation. I then sent Shaman a copy of the test results for him to forward to a doctor he knew in Hong Kong, and both Peter and the doctor in Hong Kong agreed that it was a perilous but necessary operation. Finally, I decided to call Doctor Yovanka, who was one of the *sangha* members, to ask her opinion. She, too, confirmed surgery was the only option.

Armed with the opinions of all four doctors, and the information on liver water cysts I had located on the Internet, I began to prepare myself for the operation. Although not concerned about the operation itself, I will admit I was nervous about the pain I would be subjected to afterwards. I tried to distract myself from thinking about it by repeating the mantra, "I am not this body, not this mind, immortal self I am!"

Shani and Les supported me throughout the days leading up to the operation. Then, finally, the big day arrived. Now I was ready for it to be over and done with. The day before the operation Shaman flew in from Hong Kong, as he was extremely concerned and wanted to be there for me. Shani insisted she would stay with me after the operation and duly made arrangements for the children to be looked after. How she and Andrew managed during this time was beyond me. I tried hard not to feel guilty about disrupting everyone's lives.

My Master's words rang in my ears, *'You know how to give, but you must also learn how to receive. Yoga is about balance. Not too much one way or the other.'*

I received their love and care with much appreciation.

We arrived at the High Care Hospital, the same hospital outside Marbella where Coral had been treated, several hours prior to the operation, which was scheduled to take place in the evening. Shani, Shaman and Les were all by my side as I was wheeled into the theatre where the surgeon, Doctor Chamorrow, was waiting. I looked up at him and said these words that I will never forget as long as I live and, I suspect, neither will Doctor Chamorrow. "Doctor, may your hands be blessed. If I should die on the operating table please do not blame yourself but know it was my time."

He looked down at me as I lay on the trolley, a look of amazement on his face. He smiled and said no one had ever said that to him before, and then he reassured me it would go well. I think that exchange put us both at ease and, sure enough, the operation was a success and he managed to perform removal of the cyst by keyhole surgery leaving three very small scars.

When I regained consciousness in ICU, Les was leaning over me and for some unknown reason all I could say was "I love your blue eyes!" Shani and Shaman laughed and said they had spoken to the surgeon who said the most important thing now was rest and recuperation. I told them all to go and get something to eat and not to worry about me, as I had two nurses in attendance. As soon as they left the room, I became aware of the excruciating pain all over my body, a physical pain I had never experienced before, not even in childbirth. That night sleep eluded me but I fell into a deep trance and could hear sweet voices telling me things I needed to share with everyone. Later, when I had returned home, I recorded them in my diary under the heading 'Divine Truths'. This is what I wrote:

1. Life is a journey we have evolved to be in, to experience Divine Consciousness through the material.
2. The senses are given to us to experience different sensations, and these sensations when personalised, can create addictions.
3. The sensations when de-personalized create a sense of awe and understanding of the whole creative process. We see life from the point of view of a witness.
4. With that we learn that pain and pleasure are similar to our inhalations and exhalations; like the waves of the ocean that swell at times and are subdued and quiet at other times.
5. This *knowing* sets us free and we realize our responsibility is to share this truth with all.
6. Once we know this, our mission becomes clear and simple: To find balance and harmony. Only then can we learn to love and serve unconditionally.
7. Once we experience this we learn to laugh through life and its incredible journey. Gratitude and grace fill us and we feel complete with "The One".

This experience moved me intensely. I felt I was in contact with a force from another dimension. When I recall this incident the emotions of that night run through me once more. Within the physical pain there lay such consolation, but words cannot adequately convey the depth of feeling and wonder of that night.

I remained in hospital for five days, and enjoyed the loving care of Les and my family. On returning home I felt the miracle that was life, and I was overwhelmed with gratitude. However, while recovering in my bed all manner of thoughts began to course through me. I was not afraid of dying but what I was now concerned with was how I would live. I had immersed myself in the joy of service and yet my personal time was becoming filled by being with Les. I had gone through all of this before in my marriage to Shanky. What was I to learn this time? Did I really need to go through another relationship? Something in my soul was crying out for something much more, but what? While Shaman was with me, I felt a sense of strength and security from his powerhouse of energy. From Shani I received all the unconditional love I needed, and it brought back memories of our close-knit family, of what we had before Shanky left his body. I once more became confused about my feelings towards Les. I needed time alone to think, so I called him and broke away for the third time. I later wrote in my diary:

Oh, no! I did it again! Words like, 'he's too weak for me. He's not warm with my family as Shanky was. He's not my type! But he's so kind and gentle and I LOVE that!' Ugh! These words kept spinning like wheels in my mind. I want to serve but how can I serve and love him at the same time? I was making all kinds of excuses and placing the onus on him. The truth was, I was too fearful of commitment. Too fearful of losing my freedom. These are just the wrong words to grow spiritually. What happened to my belief system of 'let go and let God?' What was Divine Will and what was my will?

Although I had once more caused him so much pain, to his eternal credit he did not give up on me. There is one incident that I must relay in order to exemplify Les's determination to win back my heart, and it is one that we now both consider as being a clear indication - proof, if you will - of how the gods have schemed and toiled to bring us together.

My birthday is in June (I am a Gemini, or as Gurudev said to me one time, 'you are a *gem in I*') and every year the members of the Integral Yoga Centre in Gibraltar would throw a surprise party for me. I say 'surprise party' but in truth my birthday parties at the Centre were the worst kept secret. I always knew they would throw a party for me on the Wednesday closest to the actual date of my birthday, but I invariably had no idea exactly what the party would include. There would always be singing and laughter but I was deliberately kept in the dark as to the programme for the event.

Every time we broke up Les would cease to attend any of the Wednesday *satsangs* at the Centre, so I did not expect to see him at my birthday party following our breakup for the second time. He was again simply too upset, so this year would be the first time he would not participate, as he had done so many times before. But I was wrong.

It was a few minutes after 6pm and my party had just begun. As usual, the Yoga hall had been decorated with balloons and streamers, and chairs had been laid out in a circle with a large chair reserved for me at the side against the wall. The centre of the hall had been cleared for the various performers who had consented to sing or dance for me (everyone was always so kind and really made me feel special on my birthday!) and all I had to do was sit back, relax and enjoy the show. The hall was full of people and I settled in my chair disbelieving that another year had flown by so quickly. And then the door of the hall opened and everyone turned to see Les walking slowly in, clutching a large bouquet of flowers.

The compere for the evening, Lilian 'Lakshmi' Shaw, stopped in mid-sentence and, somewhat surprisingly, said to Les, "Ah, there you are! We were waiting for you. It will be your turn to speak in a moment." Without saying a word, Les sat down on the floor and waited to be called. I glanced at him, he looked nervous and I became concerned at what he was about to say and do. A few minutes later, Lakshmi invited Les to the centre of the hall, as the time had come for him to contribute to the evening's festivities. I was completely unaware whether his appearance was part of the programme or not, so I watched him approach me, growing more apprehensive with each step he took.

Offering me the bouquet of flowers he proceeded to pour his heart out. Right there in front of everyone, as if a scene from some romantic movie. "I want to spend the rest of my life with you," he said aloud so that all could hear, "I want to make you laugh every day. You are the love of my life..."

I was in shock. Several people in the hall began to cry. He promised undying, unconditional love - a true outpouring of his feelings for me. I was speechless and could only thank him for the flowers. When he finished, he turned around and walked back to his seat on the floor. The hall had fallen silent but then Lakshmi asked for the next person to come to the centre to perform for me and the show went on.

At the end of the party I walked past where he was sitting and whispered to him that his words had changed nothing. He caught my hand and asked if I would have dinner with him. Much to my surprise I found myself consenting to his proposition although I made it clear to him he could not consider it a date and, accordingly, we would not get back together afterwards. He agreed to my terms and a short while later we were sitting opposite each other across a table in a restaurant we had frequently dined at on our date nights.

Over dinner he told me why he had decided to arrive unannounced at my birthday party bearing a large bouquet of flowers, and why he had spoken those words of love to me so openly, so publicly. He said the whole episode had been bizarre, as if guided by the Hand of the Divine.

He finished work early that day, as he had to leave Gibraltar to deal with a technician who was due at his apartment to install a new Internet connection. On the drive home he suddenly had a vision of himself arriving at the Yoga Centre, walking into the hall and presenting me with flowers for my birthday, but he dismissed the vision on the basis there was not enough time. There was simply no way he could go home, deal with the technician and then rush to a florist to buy the flowers, cross the border into Gibraltar (there was invariably a queue of cars to enter Gibraltar in the evening resulting in lengthy delays) and then get to the Centre before the birthday party finished at 7.30pm. However, despite his best efforts to resist it, the vision persisted in his mind and he was forced to wrestle with the idea, firstly reasoning there was insufficient time, and secondly questioning whether he had the courage to go through with it. He compared his dilemma to that of the character of Benjamin in the movie 'The Graduate' who made a desperate run to the church where Elaine, the girl he was madly in love with, was about to get married to someone else! Could Les proclaim his love to me in such a public manner, and what would those at the party think of him - and me?

And then, Les said, he received the first sign. As he approached his apartment building he noticed a large van had been parked across the gate leading to the underground parking area and barring him access to his dedicated parking space. Instead he was forced to park his car in one of the public spaces in front of the building, which had been laid out at an angle to the kerb so that when he drove into one of them his car was actually facing in the direction of Gibraltar. This made him think.

He had never been prevented from entering the underground parking area before so why now, why this particular day? So, in his words, Les made a deal with the Divine. He said, 'OK. If you want me to go through with this then you must give me several more signs. Firstly, the technician must finish his work no later than 5pm (remember, the party was due to begin at 6pm). Secondly, I must get to the florist before it closes and there must be no other customers so that I can quickly buy the flowers and head to the border. Thirdly, there must be no queue to get into Gibraltar, and lastly, there must be a parking space right outside the Yoga Centre (parking anywhere near the Yoga Centre was always problematic so this seemed quite a challenge!)

Having made the deal he then entered his apartment building and within minutes the technician arrived and began work on the Internet installation. Les waited anxiously, watching him work and keeping an eye on the time. At 4.55pm the technician announced he had completed the installation and Les suddenly realised the Divine had agreed to the deal. Now it hit him; he would have to turn the vision into reality and he became extremely nervous at the prospect of entering the hall and publicly proclaiming his love for me. It seemed that, even though there were still hurdles to jump, his misgivings that there would not be enough time were about to be dispelled leaving only the question of whether he had the courage to go through with it.

He quickly paid the technician for the work and rushed back to his car. It was 5pm and he had one hour to get to the florist, drive the 25 minutes to the border, cross into Gibraltar and find a parking space near the Yoga Centre. Despite the first sign being granted, to Les it still appeared impossible to get to the Yoga Centre on time, and the closer he got to Gibraltar the more nervous he became.

Then the second sign was granted. He got to the florist with five minutes to spare and there were no other customers. Having picked up the flowers he then had to cross into Gibraltar. A miracle. No queue.

As he approached the Yoga Centre his heart began beating faster and faster. There was just one sign remaining, and there it was. The perfect parking space right across the street from the entrance to the Yoga Centre. And it was the only space available. The time was a few minutes after 6pm. The Divine had kept to the deal. Now he had to do his part. And he did it. Just like a scene from a movie. Everything had worked like clockwork, and Les told me over dinner that it was the clearest and most profoundly convincing evidence of the existence of God he had ever experienced.

We didn't get back together that evening. It took a while longer. What did happen was that we became friends again, we started talking and, more importantly, we both realised we had been actors in a Divine movie. God had once more worked his magic around us.

Oops! There will be a third - and last time, as I finally got the message. I needed to let go and follow my heart. I could no longer resist God's will. And when someone writes a poem and romantically recites it to you, how *can* you resist?

The Truth

I see it in my lover's eyes
The sparkling windows to a gentle soul
Such tenderness, which can't disguise the inner strength
That lends itself in times of strife
To bolster up my lowly spirit.
Then, at length, appreciation comes back to life
And I anchor in her sheltering arms safe at last
From storm-tossed seas so dark without.
While nestling there she's softly soothing,
Gently moving her hand across my furrowed brow,
I can but smile and cast away
Whatever the seeds of doubt about
The truth may deign to dim the light of endless love
And stifle the warmth of her infectious laughter.
Fresh colours added to my day,
The spot-lit and dappled canvas framed

Upon the endless cold and shaded grey-toned walls
To catch the eye and draw one near
A haven that brings the gallery
Alive as the lasting pulse beats ever faster.
In unison we sing the song of life out loud,
In harmony our voices rise
With each perfect rhyme so giving vent
To ingrained feelings engraved so deeply in stone.
And then as one our bodies move,
Our hands reach up with such emotion
To grasp God's precious gift of joy with hearts of youth.
And what we feel is not a lie
The beauty is real and heaven sent -
In my love's sweet and tender devotion
There lies abiding and absolute truth.

(From *The Long Journey* - a book of poems written by Les Roberts)

Chapter 6
Epilogue – The Awakening

Diary entry - 11th November 2014:

Les left for Tanzania today. I miss him, but at the same time love my space. He has been such a gift in my life. God, you are so loving to me. I discarded this gift three times and, in your kindness, you taught me about love and your plan. Who can know it? Who can even try to understand the workings of karma? I am just grateful. Grateful that I succumbed to love. I love that you work through me and I finally truly know this. I love how you work through everyone and everything! But alas, only few recognize this. Surrendering to you, Lord of Love, is the most joyful act. Free from mind stuff, just flowing with what comes and not judging myself constantly, and not listening to the chit chatter of judgement towards me. And I nearly threw it all away thinking spirituality meant a life alone. With Les, my spirit has flown to new levels of joy! With a heart content and consoled from the pain of losing Shanky, I feel energised, alive again and I can serve even more! When one is overflowing with bitter-sweet love all one can do is share it! These past few months/years have been so full. So full of work, joy, laughter and love! Everything blossoming into the spring of my new life. SIS, the charity, has snowballed and we have been able to serve all over the world! The word is spreading! Yoga isn't about becoming a teacher or a Guru; Yoga is living each moment with the Divine essence that is *us*. What joy to be able to lift someone from sadness, anger, fear, and take them to knowledge of the Self. I am overwhelmed that we can actually make a difference to someone's life! As Les always says, *'If one soul is touched, the journey is worth the taking.'* This year has been a year of celebration. It is the year of Gurudeva's Centennial. We managed to surpass our goal of 100 good deeds in his name to two hundred and forty deeds, all documented in gratitude to the knowledge he shared so freely and lovingly with us! My brother Maj is free from cancer, and so is Les! My brother David and son Shaman have so generously paid to build a second floor to my home! So many visitors have graced us with their presence. Mataji performed a blessing ceremony for Les (Anand) and I in the Yoga hall. We had two witnesses, Shani and Andrew. I couldn't stop crying from the emotion of love that heartfelt ceremony projected. Sanjay, my nephew, graced our home for three months and stayed on for my 60th birthday. It was such fun to have him around. Every morning he would get up and perform a *puja*. I also received an accolade at Yogaville for services to humanity in July. Totally unexpected! Our family went on a Mediterranean cruise. What a trip! The grandkids tell me it is their favourite holiday. Les surprised me by organizing a long weekend away to Assisi in Italy. The one place I always wanted to visit. We sang *'Make me a channel of your Peace'* along the cobbled streets of this charming, spiritual town. We felt like children meeting the Son of God when we approached the places where St. Francis worshipped. What a year! I am rambling on as gratitude fills my being. I must go to sleep now. Tomorrow I am training twenty-two people for their Hatha exam.... Goodnight diary, goodnight God, Goodnight Universe, goodnight *sanghas*, goodnight family, goodnight Life! How much I love you all. May all be filled with peace and joy, love and Light! May this joy be spread to all those in pain and suffering and offer them relief...

Diary entry - 3rd June, 2015: A poem written after meditation

Who am I?

By Nalanie Harilela Chellaram

I watch myself,
Who is this that I am watching?
Who is the One that watches?
Who am I?

I hear countless thoughts rattling in my mind.
Some good, some bad, some with no meaning.
When I watch these thoughts, they do not control me.
When I become my thoughts, they persecute me.
Who am I?

I watch the pleasant thoughts. They take me to a good place.
Problem starts when I cannot stay there.
I stress to stay there. With patience I let that go too.
Who am I?

I watch my negative thoughts. They take me to a depressed place.
I struggle to get out. I pray and ask for help.
With patience and compassion, they leave me.
Who am I?

I watch my thoughts that are dull and meaningless.
They make me feel dull and lifeless.
I become anxious, confused and lose direction.
Who am I?

I now watch the One who watches.
I do that with my thoughts.
I only hear my thoughts and they become strangers.
Who am I?

I breathe in deeply and hold my breath.
For a split second there is nothing!
I feel warm and safe. I experience peace.
Who am I?

I watch my thoughts. They watch me.
I observe a vibration in the silence.
My body tingles. Nothing moves.
I just feel a flow of energy within me.
Love, Joy, Peace, Light.
I am not me. Then who am I?

I am the One who watches.
I am Awareness. I am Consciousness.
That is who I am.
Sivoham, Sivoham, Sivoham.

Diary entries – July to August 2016

July 24th: Shaman, Hersha, Indi and Shahan are here all summer! I have taken a month off just to have this precious time with them. Eager to have time to truly bond with the grandchildren.

July 26th: Got a phone call from Hong Kong. Minal crying on the phone. My sister Mira is dying! She said Ramesh and Sanjay are both in denial, and I need to get to Hong Kong as soon as possible. A sharp pain has again hit my heart and I know I must go immediately. I feel so torn, as the family have come all this way to spend time with us, and now I have to fly back to Hong Kong! I know Shani will look after them and Shaman is always there to take charge, like his father used to. He told me I should go, so I frantically packed a bag. Then Ramesh called and told me not to fly, as Mira will get better. I don't believe him. Minal would never utter those words unless she knew. Given her history of being so fearful at the mention of the word 'death', I know this is serious. I called Maj and told him, and he said he would also fly to Hong Kong tomorrow. Then Avisha called and confirmed what Minal had told me. So, I am definitely going.

August 4th: At the hospital, day after day we watch Mira breathing through a machine. She is heavily sedated so she does not consciously acknowledge us. But I know she sees us, feels us. Her daughters chant mantras to her constantly. We all do. Although anxious, all the family surround her with great love. I cannot help but feel modern medicine is so cruel. She is not breathing on her own. The machine is doing it for her. I watch her body deteriorate. Doctors do their best, but I see they're looking at the machine and not at her. I feel helpless, as all my family totally believe in this. I accept this with great pain. I would have liked to see Mira go gently without being tied to these horrible machines. That was her wish. But how can the family let go without doing their best? It is a dilemma for them. It is their belief system and they believe they are doing their best. For me it is clear. I pray that when my time comes, I am allowed to die at home graciously without machines. I prefer to live with quality rather than quantity. I have made this clear to my family. I want to go the way my husband did. Allowed to say goodbye. I understand there is no blame here. Just different viewpoints. No wrong or right. We all have to do what we have to do. It is the way it is. All I can do is love everyone and pray Mira goes gently to the Light, and with all the love surrounding her at her last hours, I believe she will*.

Mira passed away peacefully on the 8th August 2016.

August 2020:

So much has happened throughout the years. I am watching the play unfold, chapter by chapter. I am now 66 years of age. I have lost many loved ones in the past few years. *Sangha* members, friends, patients and another sibling - my brother Kumar, last year. Again, watching him suffer his last four months in hospital tied to machine after machine, treatment after treatment, just broke my heart. Health practitioners need to be more aware. If the patient cannot be saved then they should be allowed to transfer to hospices, palliative care centres where they can receive an understanding of the death process and be helped through the transition. So much has been written about how important it is to make sure the person dying is in a peaceful frame of mind, and to be guided by someone with the requisite knowledge. That is why priests are often called to be with people who are dying, to comfort them at the time of their death.

Death is inevitable. There is nothing to fear. We must prepare ourselves for this transition so that the journey becomes smooth. It is vital what we think at the moment of death. To quote the Bhagavad Gita:

'This is the effective yoga technique. At the time of leaving the body, mentally withdraw attention from the gates of the body into the heart area, and from there direct the prana (energy) to the head.

The gates of the body refer to the mouth, eyes, nostril, ears, anus and genitalia.

Then say aloud or think of the word 'Om' which is the manifestation of the Divine principle; you will leave the body and reach the supreme goal.'

(From *The Living Gita*: Chapter 8, Slokas 12 & 13)

Yoga practitioners may use the word *Om* or any mantra to elevate themselves. All traditions have their own prayers or chants. What is important at the time of death is to pass from this world to the next by allowing the last breath to be a letting go; a peaceful, loving moment. According to Buddhist texts it is difficult for the soul that is withdrawing from its body to be surrounded by wails and cries of sorrow from loved ones. Such noise pulls the soul back into the suffering body, only to suffer more physical pain.

Death has become my friend. Every morning when I wake up and sense my breathing, I wonder at the glory of the story of life. When I say 'glory', I include both the good times and the bad times we must experience while we are alive. One cannot exist without the other. A Rabbi once prayed, *'Lord without you there would be no me. Without me, there is no you.'*

We can compare life to a cosmic dance where we learn one step at a time until we master that step, and then we continue to learn the sequence of steps until we master the entire dance. With the choreographer's direction, with love and service in our hearts, we can perform collectively, as one, for the benefit of the world, our audience. We would no longer be in isolation, separated from one another by prejudice and the mistaken impression of our individuality. But rather we would enjoy our mutual connection to the collective consciousness. As we dance together to benefit our world, in that dance we are one.

And what about the *sanghas*? Without exception they have developed into beacons of light, and many of the members are now teaching Yoga all over the globe, spreading the word that goodness, kindness, love and compassion are the way forward. They are actively promoting the tenet there is only *one* truth, and that of the wisdom of love and understanding, and it does not matter which path we choose so long as we get there - so long as we *realise* that one truth.

It is such a gift to observe the spiritual teachings handed down by my Master are now being spread to all the corners of the earth. We need to look after each other; we need to care for our world and respect Mother Nature. We have abused her enough, and this is possibly why we have been forced to endure the ravages of the Covid-19 pandemic. It is our Karma.

During the periods of lockdown enforced by governments around the globe, so many were confined to their homes believing that death lurked just outside their doors. As a consequence some developed severe anxiety. Stress levels rose dramatically, incidents of domestic violence and suicide increased to record levels. And yet many others welcomed lockdown as a time to reflect on our world, and on themselves. Several weeks following the initial lockdown, nature began to shine as it was given the opportunity to slowly return to its pristine state, its condition before human intervention. Pollution of the air, the burning of trees, the devouring of her land and poisoning of her waters - all had temporarily ceased. Such intervention was based purely on greed and entirely unsustainable, and in a matter of days it all had to stop.

But have we learnt from the experience? Are we learning? Must life constantly produce bad, even evil, situations so that we can value what is good? Must we yearn for the 'good old days' only when we are forced to endure fearful new ones? Is it not common sense to care for each other and to treasure the earth, which has allowed us to experience so much in life? What is the point of selling our souls for a few pieces of silver?

And what about my family? My grandchildren are growing up all too quickly! The two eldest granddaughters, Tara and Natasha, have blossomed into beautiful and talented women, and are both forging careers for themselves in England. They both have fond memories of Shanky they can cherish and carry with them through life. We all have, and these keep Shanky very much alive in our hearts.

Our darling Talia has also reached her teenage years. As I write this she has just celebrated her thirteenth birthday, which is quite a miracle - the doctors said she would not survive beyond childhood. She walks and talks, in fact she is learning to understand and speak in both English and Spanish. She is very short for her age but her tiny frame is somehow endearing, as she more than compensates for her small stature by having a character larger than life!

Indira is our little 'Disney Princess'. She is a bundle of energy with a heart overflowing with love. Shahan reminds me so much of Shaman as a child, full of ideas and fun. He constantly looks for ways to make us laugh from the depths of our being.

Shaman and Hersha are flourishing in Hong Kong and spend much of their time working for the community through a charity they established called "The YAMA Foundation". Shani and Andrew have gone through their gains and their losses over the years, handling both with innovation, acceptance and positivity. I am in awe of their resolve, and I have witnessed how life has rewarded them with many gifts - *manna from heaven.*

My Mom is still with us although she has dementia and drifts in and out of this world. She is peaceful in her world and this we feel is a gift. My brother David was recently diagnosed with cancer, another victim of what seems to be the *Harilela Curse.* For some reason our family is prone to cancer, as many cousins and other extended family members have succumbed to it over the years. And cancer returned to torment Maj following Kumar's passing. They were more than brothers, almost twin souls, and their love for each other was so very strong. And yet Maj has remained extremely positive, and is determined to once more fend off this most terrible of diseases. Maj and I have shared many meaningful hours together as we witnessed the deaths of our siblings, and we have bonded again just as we were as children.

But cancer doesn't always have things its own way. A short while following Vijay's passing, Kantu was diagnosed with breast cancer, and my Aunt Sandy underwent treatment for stage four cancer. Mercifully both have survived and are now totally clear, thereby giving us hope.

Through her courage and determination, and with the love and devotion of her husband Sunil, my incredible sister Lavina – we call her 'Lavi' – is living life to the full, defying medical opinion that she would not recover from the stroke she suffered when only 38 years of age.

And Les? Wow! All I can say is that I am thrilled we got back together that third time! Our love grows by the day! During the Coronavirus lockdown, we cherished the time we had - using the time constructively and creatively, and laughing every day, just as he promised we would at my birthday party. That is one of the secrets to a successful relationship - see the bright side, see the light side and never go to sleep angry with your partner. We never argue, preferring to 'agree to disagree' on any differences of opinion we may have. Now Les and I work together. He is as determined as I am to spread the teachings so he spends hours recording and editing my talks. We get up each morning with gratitude in our hearts, and we always close the day by holding hands and thanking our Lord of Love for each other. We don't know how much time we will have together, but however much time we are given we will consciously make each day matter.

Shanky remains on my mind and in my heart, and he will always be a part of me. I talk about him frequently and am blessed to be with someone who totally understands this.

In closing, my message to the world is this: Please be kind to each other. Please practise gratitude and forgiveness. Appreciate everything that comes your way, and 'surf through the waves', both the highs and the lows. Savour each and every moment. And don't put off till tomorrow what you can do today. It is too late when we die.

Love is the magic that keeps us all alive!

Postscript
Experiences Of Acceptance And Letting Go

As we act out this play called *life* it seems almost inevitable that someone we know, someone we care for or someone we love deeply, will leave the stage never to return. Sadly, for many the pain of bereavement will be too much to bear and they will never overcome their loss. For others the healing process may last many years, possibly the remainder of their lives, but time will prove the healer we all know it can be.

For some, those equipped with the requisite knowledge and understanding, the pain can be eased and, though they will never forget their lost loved one, they can continue to function, to act in the play and move on to newer, brighter scenes.

What follows are several personal experiences written in their own words by people who, on losing a loved one, applied the knowledge and understanding that I was blessed to pass on to them. As such, their stories are remarkably similar even though their circumstances differed. We are all different. There can be varying degrees of pain depending on the nature of our relationship with the one who has left the stage. It is said that people come into our lives for either a reason, a season or a lifetime. Yet it is often the case that someone who enters our lives for a short while, for just a reason or a season, remains in our hearts for a lifetime. In keeping them there, in remembering them, their presence on the stage survives long after they have physically left it.

Experience No.1

By Turttu Balson

Fourteen years ago, on a beautiful sunny summer morning, I had just dropped my two small granddaughters at their nursery after having them stay with me for the weekend, and was on my way to their home to have a coffee with my daughter, their mother, who was waiting for me. But when

I walked into the house there was a strange silence, which made me feel uncomfortable. I called out to my daughter who was nowhere to be seen, so I walked out to the terrace thinking that she must be out in the garden. And then I saw a kind of large 'doll' floating in the pool.

There is very little I recall from those first moments when I realised the doll was my daughter's swollen body covered with hundreds of flies. That minute my heart froze and I stopped existing emotionally, and I became locked into a dark room for years to follow. Eventually, the unimaginable truth became reality and my body went into an auto-drive as I started to make all the necessary arrangements. I telephoned her husband, who was working in London, and broke the news to him.

Death and mortality are difficult subjects and even more so when you have to explain them to two very young girls, just two and five years old at the time, who are asking why their mother has died by sudden heart failure. Can't we get her a new heart? Why can't we take her out from that box (coffin) so she can come back home?

After a very solemn and sombre funeral just with the two little ones, their father and me, my life took a new turn. I had become Mama to my two small granddaughters, a role I fulfilled for years afterwards, taking the role of the mother, as their father had to carry on working in London and only returning to Spain for weekends.

All I focused on now was to love, cherish and balance these two small souls that had been left in my care. They were my precious inheritance from my daughter. Then eleven months following the loss of my only child, my mother died, and now the only family I had left was my two little granddaughters.

At times our own light goes out and the darkness falls and fills our whole being. For years, I was in that darkness without light.

Then one day my very dear friends Ole and Kim, seeing my sadness, convinced me to meet 'this yoga woman' who, they told me, is incredible and can help me to rekindle my light. At first I resisted, as I did not want to get involved with some kind of *guru* who wanted to sell me the way to heaven. However, eventually, I gave in and went with them to a meeting called a *satsang,* and there I met Nalanie Harilela Chellaram.

I can still remember very clearly that first meeting, now twelve years ago, sitting at the back of this dark room with lots of people all humming something in a very strange language! Then in walked this beautiful Indian woman who was glowing with love and light. I listened to her but cannot recall much about what she said, only that a strange peace filled me during her talk. Little did I know then how dramatically this woman was going to change my life with her teaching of truth, knowledge and bliss, and how she was going to give me a key to get out from my darkness and turn my tears into diamonds

A few years later, after I had become a regular attendee at her *satsangs* and a firm admirer not only of Nalanie's sincere love and selfless service to humanity but also of her huge knowledge and understanding of life, death and universe, I was ready to take the next step and undertake her course in The Yoga Sutras and Hatha Yoga.

I never had time for bereavement, everything was bottled up inside of me so when I heard Nalanie's teaching of The Yoga Sutras, their truth and knowledge gradually and slowly dropping the illusions, sorrow and sadness in me, peeling off the layers and bringing an awareness and understanding of who I am, with it came a new freedom, acceptance and an inner peace like I never felt before. It was a spiritual heart attack that changed my life forever.

Ever since I have practised the 'eight limbs of yoga' and experienced the *union*, with early morning silence, self-observation and meditation in nature, which connects me to the supreme energy that makes me feel humble and non-judgemental, and fills me with awareness and knowledge that I am not this body, not this mind but immortal soul I am. It is such freedom, harmony and joy to experience!

A *Puja* is a ceremony, a beautiful spiritual offering of light, flowers, water and food to the Divine. Nalanie offered to perform this for my late daughter to celebrate and honour her memory when I told her that we never had any kind of memorial service after her funeral. This most touching event of blessing and love by Nalanie brought a final peace and closure to the hearts of my granddaughters and me, resting our beloved soul to her eternal peace. Words can never adequately express my deep gratitude to Nalanie for giving us the experience of the *Puja* and its immense emotional benefits that have endured ever since.

After all the years of darkness, the light shines now permanently in my heart making my life peaceful, easeful and useful.

> *'Truth is One, Paths are Many.'*
> (Swami Satchidananda)

Dear Nalanie, thank you for guiding and loving me all these years and for giving me the right key to unlock it all.

Experience No.2

By Georgia Bizzell

Tara: I honestly believed my heart would stop beating when hers did. We were best friends and were each other's soul sisters. I couldn't imagine life without Tara; we were G&T! What is a Gin without a Tonic?

It's impossible to think back to the days after Tara's death as individual events. All days seemed to roll into one long nightmare that I couldn't wake up from. The pain was excruciating. I couldn't accept what was happening. It didn't make sense. I had so many questions that nobody seemed to have the answers to.

Death was new to me. When you hear about the different stages of grief it's hard to imagine that you will recognize the emotions as 'normal', because nothing about the situation was normal to me. Denial came and went quickly; I feel as though I have always been a very pragmatic person, which probably helped. Even if I didn't want what was happening, I could accept that it was. I recognize now, that I was angry at the wrong people and even at her at one stage, for leaving me behind. I was angry when people started going back to work and continuing with their lives. My world felt as if it had stopped. It obviously carried on, unphased by my chaos. I was even angry at times for existing. Bargaining was a very strange emotion that I struggled with. I knew that Tara wasn't coming back, but I just wanted one last hug, kiss, or drive, one last lunch, one last everything.

I wanted to see her. I looked forward to sleeping, because at least there was a chance that I would see Tara again in my dreams. And I did!

You don't sail through the emotions in any sequential order. I was depressed while experiencing all these other foreign feelings. Depression crept up on me. Almost like a shadow I tried to escape from, but it was always there, lingering. The inner turmoil was exhausting, I wanted to do "nice things" that T "would have wanted" but if I laughed, I felt guilty. I thought I shouldn't have fun if she wasn't there.

I saw a grievance counsellor who strangely reminded me of Tara. She was warm and smiley. Or it may have been that I was so desperate to find her, that I saw her in everyone. We met up once or twice a week and talked about good times when Tara was alive, and I'd call them 'the better days'. My friends and I would always talk about Tara, but it was refreshing to speak to someone who had no connection to her. I would offload, and together we'd laugh and cry, and I'd walk out of the clinic feeling a lot lighter, as if I could breathe again.

I don't have children of my own but having them around helped with healing. You are forced to laugh and play. A couple of days after Tara's death, my niece Jayda and nephew Byron were at the apartment I was staying in. Just before they left, Jayda, aged 4, made this strange statement with no prompt or prior conversation on the topic: "Ticky and Tacky, Jackie the Backie, Jim with two noses and Jo with the bow". I was puzzled. My mum began crying and went on to tell me the story of the Paper Dolls. It's about a little girl who makes Paper Dolls with these names. They go on all these amazing adventures, until a naughty boy comes along with a pair of scissors. He cuts them up and says they are gone forever. They aren't gone though; as the Paper Dolls join together again in the little girl's memory and live on forever. Although not at the time, this story later gave me some sort of faith. It was hard to understand that my 4-year-old niece with all the innocence in the world could have such a complex understanding of the events and know that this story would give me hope.

I was brought up as a Catholic but hadn't prayed in years. My mum asked me to have a session with Nalanie. It feels like a bit of a blur now, but I remember her being so happy. I remember thinking, 'she doesn't know why I'm here. She wouldn't be this happy if she knew my best friend had just died.' She talked about the body being a shell, or a vehicle, that this life wasn't the only life. It was Tara's time, and 'He' had other jobs for her. I wanted to believe her, but I couldn't. It took me a lot of time to come to terms with this. I was too concerned with my own needs and wanting T back in my life.

Nalanie encouraged me to write my feelings down to get them off my chest. She also encouraged me to speak at the funeral, if I could. The funeral is another day that I remember little of, but I managed to write and say my piece. It is hard to believe that as I was going through such a dark time, such a positive message shone through me. I didn't recognize myself, or where I had conjured up this strength from. Sydney (Tara's sister) and Livie (Tara's cousin) and I all spoke at the Mass. Our speeches were videoed, and when looking back, we could see a bright white orb on all of us as we were speaking. Nalanie said this was either in the shape of a butterfly, or a clover - for luck.

I'm so grateful for my family and the group of friends I have. It sounds like a cliché, but without them, I don't know where I'd be today. It's funny that when you grieve such a significant loss, you feel as though the only person you think can help you is the very person that you are grieving for. I thought about the things Tara would say, "just take a deep breath and repeat it's going to be fine, and eventually it will be". She was right. My friends also went to see Nalanie, we attended the weekly talks in the Yoga Centre, which I believe were vital to our healing. We were all in it together. We were a real sisterhood, bound by something that most 25-year-olds shouldn't have to experience.

On what would have been Tara's 25th birthday, we held a huge party. She loved flamingos, so we had a tropical themed party booming with flowers and love and summer feels! Tara's family had requested that, rather than flowers, people donated to the Animals in Need Foundation. Over £12,000 had already been raised in her name. Tara loved celebrating and found any excuse for a party! We celebrated her birthday, which gave us another reason to do such great work with the charity. We danced and cried and truly had a night to remember.

Not long after this, I moved to the UK. I found Gibraltar too claustrophobic. Everything I saw was related to Tara and all the memories we shared. I couldn't get on with life. I'd find myself, going to a restaurant and then scrolling through our text messages to find a time when we went there, so I could reminisce. I knew this wasn't healthy or sustainable. I needed a change of scenery, a new beginning.

One thing that was important to me was to stay at her parents' home. I was so close to Tara and stayed at her home often. So, I wanted to sleep in her bed. It sounds strange, but waking up and her not being there, as sad as it was, gave me comfort. I could still feel her. I'd think back to days with her waking up in the morning and us getting ready at her dressing table, drinking the Twining's English Breakfast Tea that T's mum, Paola would make us in the morning, and listening to our favourite songs. It was the same, except Tara wasn't there.

Fast-forward a couple of months and my mentality on life changed so much. Even something as minor as 'saving things'. For example, I would save a candle for a special occasion, even though when I die, the candle isn't coming with me. So now I make sure to light my candles and enjoy them! I make a conscious effort to live in the present. Similarly, concerning my tattoos, this body isn't coming when I go, so I'm going to enjoy it while I have it! My favourite flower is a lotus, not just because they are beautiful, but I loved the idea that they could be made in muddy waters and still bloom so perfectly. We called Tara 'la flor' because flowers seemed to follow her. I asked her to draw a lotus for me and I had it tattooed on my back. It means everything to me, she was always with me, even when she wasn't!

Was all of this a lesson? Now I realise how precious life is, and that nothing is guaranteed. I make more of an effort with those around me, and although I don't want to be impatient, I also don't want to 'waste' time. There are so many things about life that I love. I'm grateful for all of it, especially for things I wouldn't have been concerned with before.

Despite anything that happens in our lives, the sun will rise again each morning. I'm finding that I'm more deeply connected with all the beautiful wonders of nature and spending a lot more time outside. I'm practising Yoga and meditation as part of my daily routine and I feel as if I'm on a spiritual high. I never want to come down! In my most magical meditation experience to date, I felt as if I was rooted to the earth and my body was hollow but made up entirely of stars. Nalanie explained that this means that I'm connected with Mother Nature and the universe as well as being grounded. Tara's name in Sanskrit means 'star'. Is this just another coincidence?

As people we often think about what we are lacking. Through all the pain and suffering endured, I have also gained a deeper understanding of life and a level of gratitude I did not have before. We are constantly changing, shifting, with the phases of the moon! There is no doubt that Tara is by my side and always will be. I am excited about seeing her again, not just in my dreams, but in my next life - whatever it may be. I used to say I can't wait, but I can wait now. I know it will come at the right time.

Experience No.3

By Yolanda 'Chitra' Alvarez

The object of listening to the teachings over and over again is that, some day, they will be put into practice. It is almost a certainty that one day life will throw a situation at you whereby you will need and can use the teachings to get you through it, and hopefully learn from them first time round.

Tuesday, 6th April 2010 was my birthday. I was at home after a tiring day at work and talking to Nalanie who had called to wish me a happy birthday. I recall I mentioned to Nalanie that I was ready to serve. I remember all too well her words to me, "Well, Chitra, ask and you shall receive!" Little did I know that only days later I was going to be given the chance to serve and, boy, I did not expect what was coming! On Friday, 9th April, I received a call from my sister to tell me Mum had suffered a stroke.

For as long as I can remember, Mum had suffered from heart problems, and she frequently ended up in the ICU at the hospital in Gibraltar with palpitations. So we were accustomed to spending time with her in hospital, often for a few days or a week, and even occasionally having to take her to London for treatments, etc. She even survived a valve replacement just a couple of years before she passed away. Yet, despite this 'history' and my sister and I being used to Mum being in hospital, somehow that day I felt a dread that something really bad was going to happen.

I went immediately to the hospital and when I arrived at the ICU I saw my Mum lying unconscious, and the doctor proceeded to tell my sister and I that in stroke cases the first 72 hours are critical. I panicked because my dread was starting to be come true and all kinds of emotions flashed through me. I broke into an anguished cry, my whole body was telling me to prepare myself and suddenly I couldn't think straight.

When Mum regained consciousness she was half paralysed. The doctor told us she had suffered severe damage to her brain and therefore needed physiotherapy to help her recover. Unfortunately, due to the severe damage to her brain, she was lucid only part of the time and not at all so at other times. As a result the physiotherapist was unable to work with her to increase her mobility. I knew then the long, difficult and challenging journey had begun for me.

I recall that when I was informed of the severity of her condition I experienced a panic attack. A fear of what was going to happen, of anguish and despair. My whole life had collapsed and I didn't know what to do. I felt alone and vulnerable. I had recently moved in with my ailing Dad thinking it only a temporary arrangement, and now what? I had mixed feelings of selfishness, wanting to go back to my own apartment and refuge, and also of guilt because my Dad needed my help, and a sense of being powerless because I didn't know how to deal with this situation. I sank into a deep sadness. Sad that my Mum was extremely ill, and in my heart I knew she would never get better. A flood of emotions overtook me, causing me a lot of stress and grief.

I believe that, at some point shortly afterwards, acceptance of the situation came to me, and I started thinking more clearly how to manage myself and the circumstances I was now having to deal with. I decided that I had to put my life on hold and not to set any time limit in order to avoid any further stress. I also became stronger and even though I was not the elder sister I realised I had to make important and difficult decisions for the benefit of everyone, including myself.

I became calmer and clearer about my purpose. Following consultation with both my Dad and his doctor, the first decision I took was that it was time for me to move back to my apartment. My Dad's doctor agreed and actually recommended it, as Dad needed space too, space to become stronger and more independent. I also decided to talk to the doctor at the hospital to see if my Mum could be moved to a different ward. My sister is a nurse and at the time of Mum's release from the ICU she took the decision to have her in the ward she worked in so that she could take care of her, but it proved a bad decision, as she got stressed out and it became a challenge for her, both mentally and physically.

I consider myself blessed and looked after because the day before I decided to talk to the doctor about moving Mum to a different ward, my sister's Department Head made the decision for me and I was able to avoid any confrontation and argument with my sister.

My next decision was to honour and take care of myself. I had been putting both my body and mind under a lot of stress, and now I had back pains and I knew intuitively that my adrenal glands were being overworked as a result of all the pressure. At the time I lived across the border in Spain so by the time I finished visiting Mum at the hospital and drove over I would arrive home between 9.00pm - 9.30pm, and then the following morning get up at 6.00am to go to work back in Gibraltar. So I decided to enjoy my home when I was there, enjoy and focus on my work without feeling any guilt or remorse, and when I was at the hospital with Mum just to be there for her. I knew one day her time would be up and I wanted to enjoy every minute with her, embracing the time we had been given before she left her body.

The next nineteen months were extremely painful and difficult, and yet at one point I remember my cousin telling me that, although she knew the pain I was going through, she could see reflected on my face the peace I had inside of me. I recalled one of Nalanie's talks that I had attended at the Yoga Centre, when she spoke about being in pain and at the same time being at peace. I didn't understand then, how can a person be in pain and have peace at the same time? Now, apparently, I was experiencing it, I was living the teachings and putting them into practice without even knowing it! I firmly believe that it was my acceptance of the situation and making the most of the time I had with my Mum that did it.

Mum too was going through her own emotions. Sometimes she was sad, or angry, irritable, embarrassed that her daughter had to bathe her, etc. She felt so lost at times. I knew she was very sacred and my heart kept breaking to see her in that state. I did my utmost to reassure her and somehow pass on my strength to her, but I don't know if I succeeded. I tried chanting to her, telling her jokes or even just holding her hand. I cherished every moment I had with her, and the knowledge one day I was going to lose her hurt me immensely.

It was going to be her birthday on 11th November 2011. She was going to be 75 years old, but a week earlier she informed me she did not want to celebrate her birthday, she didn't want any fuss. I suspect she must have known she was dying. She also told me that what saddened her most was that I was on my own. It took all the strength I had to reassure her that I never felt alone. I even asked her, "don't you see how happy and independent I am?" She looked at me and said, "yes". Then I told her, "don't worry about me. I am okay and I will be okay."

I guess it was my letting go and reassuring her it was okay for her to leave her body that a week later, on 9th November 2011 she passed away, just two days before her 75th birthday.

It was very painful, as we had a special bond. And for a long time there was sadness, a great sense of loss and excruciating pain. The only way I was able to feel better was by telling myself, almost repeating it as a mantra, that I preferred this pain to seeing my Mum suffer. That thought kept me sane and helped me to go through the process of grieving, which took a while. Although people could not see it, deep inside I missed her terribly and I cried for my loss.

Letting go is not easy, either on death or separation by some other means. Sometimes we cannot see why it is happening or comprehend it, and it becomes more difficult to accept and let go. I was lucky - for me seeing my Mum in pain was not an option, and that made it easier for me to accept her passing.

Experience No.4

By Julio Alcantara

Exasperating and funny, obstinate and generous, San was my soul-mate, San was my love, San was my life. We shared laughter and pain, the sheer joy of our sons' birth and the struggle of creating a loving home for over fifty years. Yoga teachers both, it was a reasonable expectation that we would grow old together into the twilight of our lives. I took all prudent steps that my beautiful San would be safe and comfortable when the day came I would pass on. But God had other ideas; He was in need of an angel and I wasn't up to the job. San developed cancer.

One evening, three years ago, I held her hand, mini-fractions of a second later I held nothing. The sense of loss was brutal. The sheer sense of helplessness, the vulnerability of impotence, the sheer depth of hopelessness enveloped my very soul. I suddenly and for the first time, understood the meaning of a broken heart. I sank into the darkness, a veritable dark swamp of grief. You move into a void, the indescribable face of emptiness. You lose your ability to think, to breathe, to feel anything but deep, deep pain. No words can really explain or describe the whole gamut of experiences and feelings that we run through. Despair. In the deep painful loneliness of the night, I screamed at God! Why her and not me? Why not recall us both together? What is the point of my life now? I prayed every night to die!

We are weaker and more vulnerable than our egos ever allowed us to see. Yet, surprisingly certainly to me, we discover an inner strength that we never could have imagined we have. When one reaches bottom, the only other way is up. In the face of that void you can choose joy and meaning. You can shed tears that she is gone or you can smile because of the love you shared. You can wallow in yesterday, in the quicksand of self-pity, or you can face tomorrow because of the love and goodness of yesterday.

As one teacher put it, we carry a huge reservoir of sadness. The pain and sadness walks with me every day; I can touch them in my heart. I never could have imagined how much I can cry and how often the pain reaches me. But, I am grateful for all the goodness my wife left behind. I am grateful for the kindness of my friends, the love of my family, the smiles of my beautiful grandsons. I am grateful for the gift of life itself, for each precious day. It seems my heart has been opened, refined like gold, so that I may daily see and experience the beauty of life, the Oneness of Creation. Through the pain I can smile again in the knowledge of God's infinite love for us, in the goodness of His plan for us, and a deep mysterious understanding that all will be well because San is His beautiful angel and her love is all around me.

Experience No.5

By Susanna 'Shanti' Alman

I was introduced to my beloved teacher and Yoga Master, Nalanie Chellaram after experiencing a miscarriage in 1993. I am eternally grateful to Nalanieji, as knowing her has changed my life forever.

Losing a child was so devastating and heart-breaking. Being a naturally nervous person, I thought that doing yoga would help me to calm down and also help me to conceive again. I also wanted to find some answers. Going to Nalanie's Hatha classes and talks really helped me to go within and to be less nervous. When I got pregnant again in 1996, just after my father had passed away, I was overjoyed. I thought this child was a gift from my father. However, it wasn't meant to be, as I suffered a second miscarriage. The emotional pain was horrendous, as I was grieving for my father and my unborn child. This was the lowest time in my life.

With a broken heart, I threw myself into Yoga and became a Yoga teacher, which helped tremendously. However, I was still obsessed with having a child. Family and friends were having babies and there seemed to be pregnant mums all around me. Then, in 1999, Nalanie and some of the Yogis from the Gibraltar Yoga Centre, went to Bali for a retreat with our beloved Guru, Sri Swami Satchidananda. He was introduced to us by Nalanieji in 1995 and in 1996 when he came to Gibraltar. This trip to Bali would change my life forever. Sri Gurudevaji gave me the spiritual name Shanti, which means peace and also initiated me by giving me my own sacred mantra. He placed his hand on my shoulder afterwards saying: "Are you peaceful now?"

When I got home I wrote him a letter about my desire to have a baby. He answered, saying: 'As you wrote God knows what is best for us. Suffering is a blessing in disguise. Accept God's will and keep your peace. If you are meant to have a baby, it will happen. Love God like you would love your baby. Serve and love your family and friends as if they were your own babies, you will experience the greatest joy of giving'.

Over the next few years, I had two more miscarriages. It was not meant to be. The only choice I had was to surrender to His will, which was a huge challenge. It wasn't easy, but it helped to have the Yoga teachings, my family, Nalanie, and also my Yoga family and friends in my life, which gave me the strength to carry on. My faith in God helped me face the pain with great strength and to accept the Divine plan.

After my fourth miscarriage at the age of 44, someone told me: " You won't be able to do the work that God has planned for you if you have a child". After hearing this, something changed in my brain and from that day forward there was no looking back. Now, at the age of 59, it is very clear that God's plan is indeed perfect, as I'm so happy with my life. It's about making the most of the life that we have been given. I'm so free to serve others, to serve my wonderful husband, my mum and Nalanieji. I am also free to travel, take singing lessons, go on Yoga Retreats and do lots of wonderful things. I have time to teach Yoga, lead chanting and meditation sessions and run Yoga teacher training courses with other teachers, which is so fulfilling and is my greatest joy and honour. There is still so much to learn and I am grateful to be a humble instrument of the Divine. The loss of my first child led me to Yoga and to the path of the Divine, being of service to Him, wherever I am needed, with a heart full of love and gratitude.

Losing four children has helped me to find myself. Someone once said that advanced Souls come to the wombs of Yogis, as they only have a little bit of Karma left to do before they are free. Thank you, beautiful babies, for choosing me as your mum, I am extremely honoured to have been with you, if only for just a short time. God bless you Dylan, Sharon, Louis and Angelina. I love you with all my heart. Thank you for helping me love so unconditionally, with a heart full of humility, gratitude and love for everyone, knowing that everything happens for a reason and that the Divine always knows what is best for us.

Experience No.6

By Les Roberts

Early one morning in 2008 I was out jogging my usual route around Gibraltar and looking forward to having a shower and a good breakfast. As I ran downhill towards my apartment I suddenly felt and heard a loud 'crack', and a bolt of excruciating pain gripped me and stopped me in my tracks. The pain came from the top of my spine fairly close to my neck and I immediately feared the worst, that I had broken one of my vertebrae, but I was completely mystified and could not understand how or why it had happened. I was only jogging downhill! And what if the vertebrae splintered and a piece of bone became trapped in my spinal chord? Could I become paralysed?

The pain was too severe so I immediately made the decision to go directly to the medical centre. There a well meaning doctor examined me and recommended I have an x-ray taken to see what the problem and the extent of any damage was. Incredibly he told me there was a long waiting list of people needing x-rays and I would have to join the queue, and it might take over a week before I could get an appointment. In the meantime he prescribed some strong painkillers as he could see I was in agony. However, I could not wait. It wasn't just the pain; it was also the 'not knowing' and the worry that made me impatient. So I walked the short distance to a private medical clinic where a sympathetic receptionist arranged an immediate appointment with one of the doctors there. I explained the situation to him and he picked up the phone and managed to get an appointment for me to have an x-ray the following day - at the same radiology department in the same local hospital that the doctor at the health centre informed me had a long waiting list! Money talks. Loudly. But I didn't care how much it would cost. I needed to find out what was wrong with me.

The doctor at the private clinic looked at the x-ray of my spine and confirmed that I had indeed fractured one of my vertebrae. He reassured me that from what he could see there was no risk of a splinter lodging in my spinal chord and causing paralysis. He prescribed more painkillers and advised me to rest. I was naturally relieved although I was also disappointed as it meant I had to stop jogging for a while. But this was just the beginning of a journey that almost cost me my life.

A few months later, now in 2009, as I stepped out of the shower one morning I glanced over my shoulder at my reflection in the large bathroom mirror and noticed a lump had developed on my shoulder blade. I have no idea what made me decide to look in the mirror as I reached for a towel. Normally I would look at the towel I am reaching for, but on this occasion I glanced behind me. I had not felt there was anything wrong with my back, as the fracture had apparently healed and I was no longer in any pain, not even a residual sensation. Now, however, something else was happening to me, which had crept up on me, as I had not felt the presence of the lump on my shoulder blade. So I went back to the medical centre and this time a different doctor to the one I had seen earlier took one look at the lump and said it resembled a fatty growth but he would send me for tests to be sure it was nothing more serious. This time I was able to have the tests carried out quickly - there was no waiting list.

What happened next could be considered almost farcical if it wasn't for the seriousness of the situation I found myself in. I was sent for a scan. The radiologist, apparently familiar with my sort of situation to the point of being blasé about it, calmly informed me that the fracture had not healed and that I had osteoporosis, which is rare in men of my age (54). He then went on to state that the lump on my shoulder blade was a malignant tumour. A double whammy. Osteoporosis and cancer. He told me to go home and 'try not to worry too much'. I thought to myself, 'please define *too much*'.

I returned to my office, closed the door and broke down in tears. This 'why me?' self-pity lasted only a few minutes. I suddenly became calm and clear, and I got down on my knees and prayed. Whatever would be, would be. I realized I had a choice. I could either spiral downwards into deep depression or I could spiral upwards and accept the Divine will. A part of me was now missing - the ability to plan ahead more than a few weeks, and I accepted that, readily and happily. It wasn't denial. It was pure acceptance. And I felt peaceful and ready to take on whatever challenges my new situation threw at me.

In the weeks that followed the administration department at the Gibraltar hospital made several attempts to refer me to a specialist surgeon in England who could perform the operation to remove my unwanted intruder, but without success. One day I mentioned my plight to Nalanie and she immediately recommended I get a second opinion and duly made an appointment for me with a specialist in Marbella, Spain. I understood how difficult this was for her, as she had recently lost her husband, Shanky, and the specialist I was going to see was the same doctor who had treated him. During the consultation with the Spanish specialist he made it clear that I could not wait and that I had to have the tumour removed immediately before it metastasized. I returned to the Gibraltar hospital one more time, to inform them that my case was now urgent. Again I was asked to return in a few days time. Enough was enough. The medical system in Gibraltar had failed me; they could not appreciate how serious my condition was. When someone is diagnosed with a malignant tumour it is not unreasonable to expect to be fast-tracked so that proper and appropriate medical attention is provided expeditiously. Now I was left with no choice. I would have to rely on private medical care, whatever it may cost. I immediately called Nalanie and through her son-in-law, Andrew, whose brother was a doctor based in the United Kingdom, she managed to make an appointment for me to see a specialist surgeon in England the following week. I returned home and booked a one-way air ticket to England and a hotel room close to the private hospital where the specialist surgeon was based.

I also called my eldest daughter, Francesca, as I needed someone with me while I underwent first the pre-op tests and then the operation. She lived in England and because we were geographically far apart we hadn't been able to spend much time together. Although she never showed it, I knew it was hard for her to see me going through this ordeal. She was a rock and never complained, and I was so grateful she was with me. The day after the operation I was discharged, and thanks to the morphine I had been given I was on a high, and I took Francesca shopping and bought her a complete outfit, including shoes, as a thank you for being with me. Looking back I have no idea how I managed that. I had just undergone major surgery but I didn't care. I was so concerned for Francesca and that she was worried about me that I forgot about the operation, and the morphine helped me to forget the pain!

To cut a long story short, the operation had gone well and the lump was sent for a biopsy, so following a few days of recuperation at my parents' home in Shropshire I returned to Gibraltar with thirty-six metal staples in my shoulder blade. Several weeks after the operation, I received a call from the specialist surgeon who had finally received the results of the biopsy on the lump he had removed. He began the call by saying he had good news and bad news and asked me which I wanted to hear first. I opted for the good news. The operation had been a complete success and he had removed all of the tumour, which had not metastasized. I was in the clear so what was the bad news? He said that if he hadn't removed it all then there would have been nothing he or anyone else could do to save me. The tumour was a rare form of bone cancer that would not respond to either chemotherapy or radiotherapy. If it had metastasized it would have killed me. I broke down for the second time, but this time it was from relief and I became acutely aware that Nalanie, when she insisted I have a second opinion, had saved my life.

The calmness I felt after I broke down the first time could also be attributed to her. She had taught me faith, to be strong in the face of adversity, and by her example to accept the will of the Divine and to surf life's waves. The peace I felt, and the acceptance of whatever will be, will be, made my 'brush with death' easy. I now look back at that period of my life and can honestly say it was exciting! There was no fear, only peace.

Over the next three years I underwent periodic tests to ensure the cancer had not returned. I also made a successful claim against the Gibraltar Health Authority for negligence that almost killed me and recovered most of the costs of the private treatment. And I also became embroiled in a dispute with members of the medical profession who insisted there was no link between the osteoporosis and the tumour. I was living proof there was. The fracture in my vertebrae and the tumour were no more than three inches apart. The fracture was the first symptom I had cancer.

Nalanie later revealed to me the conversation she had with the doctor in Marbella, which had been in Spanish so I did not understand, during that 'second opinion'. She asked him how long I would have if I did not have the tumour removed immediately. His answer was one month. I had it removed just over three weeks later. It was a close call and thanks to Nalanie I am here to tell the story.

Finally, I must mention one other thing. In 2014 my father passed away aged 94, and in March 2020 my mother was finally reunited with him. They had been married 63 years. To me, despite the sadness I feel, their passing was a blessing, as they had both suffered physically in their final years. They were both proud and, as their bodies slowly began to fail, they had lost much of their dignity. My mother was a devout Christian whose faith was unshakable and an incredible inspiration. I shall miss them terribly but my own experience, the time when I could have gone before them, taught me a great lesson. It was the time when Nalanie's teachings came alive for me and my ordeal put them to the test. I finally understood that the true Self - with a capital S - never dies. We are soul. They, my parents, though they have left their bodies, live on and not just in the hearts of those who loved them.

We will all live on and not just in the hearts of those who love us.

Appendix
Information And Bibliography

Book One – Loss: Page 10

The Mahamrityunjaya Mantra (literal translation "Great Death-conquering Mantra") also known as the *Tryambakam Mantra*:

> *oṃ tryambakaṃ yajāmahe sugandhiṃ puṣṭi-vardhanam*
> *urvārukam iva bandhanān mṛtyor mukṣīya mā 'mṛtāt*

Translation by *Sri Swami Satchidananda:*

> *We worship the all seeing one, fragrantly He nourishes us bounteously*
> *From fear of death may he set us free, to realise immortality.*

Book Three – Love: Page 163

The Chakras are part of our subtle anatomy, psychically connected to our physical bodies. The word *Chakra* means 'spinning energy' or 'wheels of energy'. There are seven main *chakras,* which correspond to our emotional dispositions. These seven points are arranged vertically along the axial channel (*Sushumna Nadi* in Hindu texts, *Avadhuti* in some Buddhist texts) from the base of the spine to the crown of the head.

Bibliography

Being Mortal   *Medicine and What Matters in the End*
by *Atul Gawande*
Profile Books Limited, London, England

Divine Grace   *Nalanie Harilela Chellaram*
Printed in Great Britain by Acorn Press Swindon Limited

The Living Gita   *The Complete Bhagavad Gita* - A commentary by
Sri Swami Satchidananda
Integral Yoga Publications, Yogaville, Virginia, USA

The Long Journey   *Les Roberts*
Dev Books, Delhi, India

The Prophet   *Kahil Gibran*
Arcturus Publishing Limited, London, England

The Tao Te Ching   *Lao Tzu* – Translation and Annotation by *Derek Lin*
Skylight Paths Publishing, Woodstock, Vermont, USA

The Tibetan Book   *Sogyal Rinpoche*
Of Living & Dying   HarperCollins Publishers, International

The Upanishads   Translated by *Eknath Easwaran*
Nilgiri Press, Tomales, California, USA

The Yoga Sutras   Translation and commentary by *Sri Swami Satchidananda*
Of Patanjali   Integral Yoga Publications, Yogaville, Virginia, USA